MOSQUITO

Jaguar

tin roof

Dionesia is a Chalupi Indian who lives in the Chaca area of Paraguay. The people in her village are mostly farmers and they make their own strings out of cactus fibers. Just like in other parts of the world, the string figures that the Chalupi make show things that are part of their everyday lives: a dragonfly, a cactus fruit, deer, a snake, a squash and, of course, a mosquito.

TAPIR

Hyacinthine MACAW

The kids in Dionesia's village didn't know many of these string games when we visited, but their mothers and grandmothers could make them all.

The Cacique—or chief—of the village was hopeful that all the kids would learn string games so they could someday teach them to *their* kids.

Dionesia   Age: 9

Hometown: Obrero, Paraguay

Pets: Dog named Tiza (Which means chalk)

Favorite Game: Marbles or swinging on the tire swing.

Most Amazing Thing She's Ever Seen: "An eclipse of the sun."

Capybara

Agave

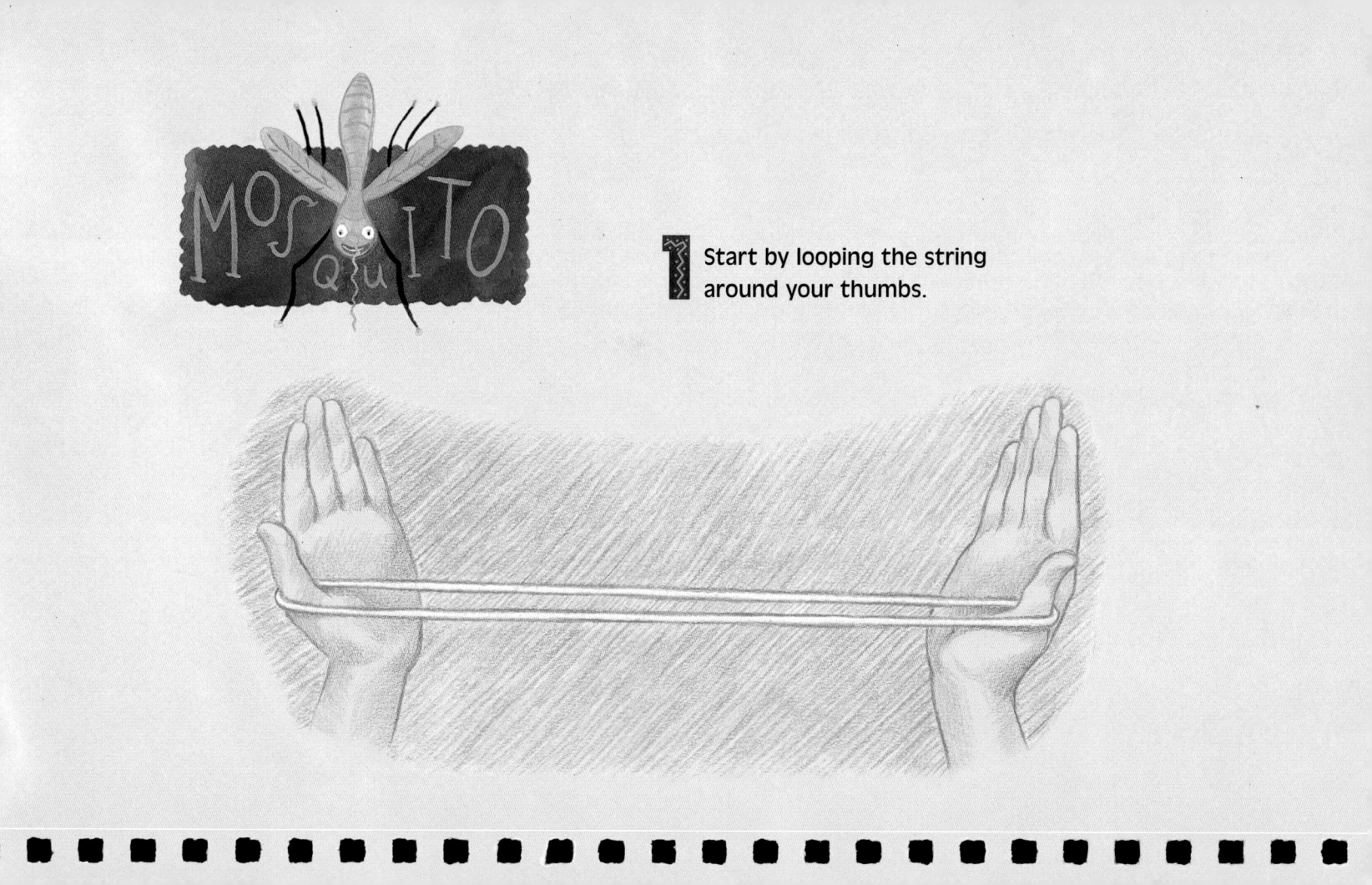

MOSQUITO

1 Start by looping the string around your thumbs.

Red marks the string you pick up next.

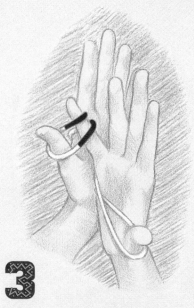

2

Wrap the string around the back of your left hand. It is still looped around each thumb.

3

Reach across with your right pinkie and pick up both pieces of string that run between your thumb and first finger.

Pull your hands apart.

 Now reach over all the strings with your left pinkie and pick up the two strings that come off your right thumb.

Pull your hands apart.

Red marks the string you pick up next.

 Squeeze the fingers of your left hand together to hold all the strings together. Use your right hand to pick up the strings that run around the back of your left hand. Pull them up over your fingers and drop them in front of your hand.

6

Pull your hands apart and you'll see the mosquito. Wiggle your pinkies and thumbs in and out to make the mosquito fly. Don't forget to buzz like a mosquito as you do this.

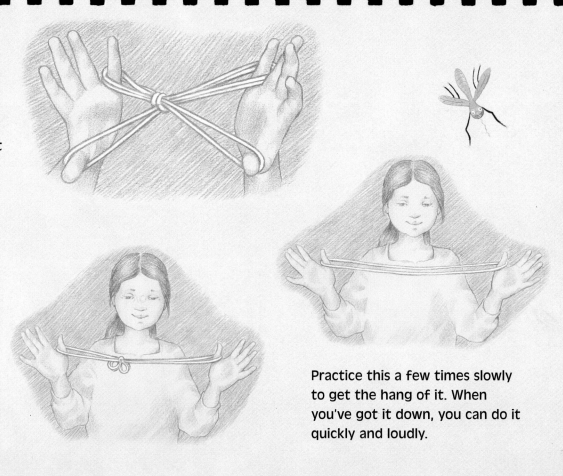

7

Now comes the good part. As soon as your audience admires your nicely buzzing mosquito, slap your hands together and shout "Got it!" Then pull your hands apart, letting the loops slip off of both pinkies. The mosquito will disappear.

Practice this a few times slowly to get the hang of it. When you've got it down, you can do it quickly and loudly.

AUSTRALIA
KOALA
Indian
ocean
Thursday island
New
Guinea
Torres
strait
Coral Sea
Ayers Rock
AUSTRALIA
ants
Perth
white
SHARK
Sydney
EMU
Melbourne
duck-billed
PLATYPUS

PALM TREE

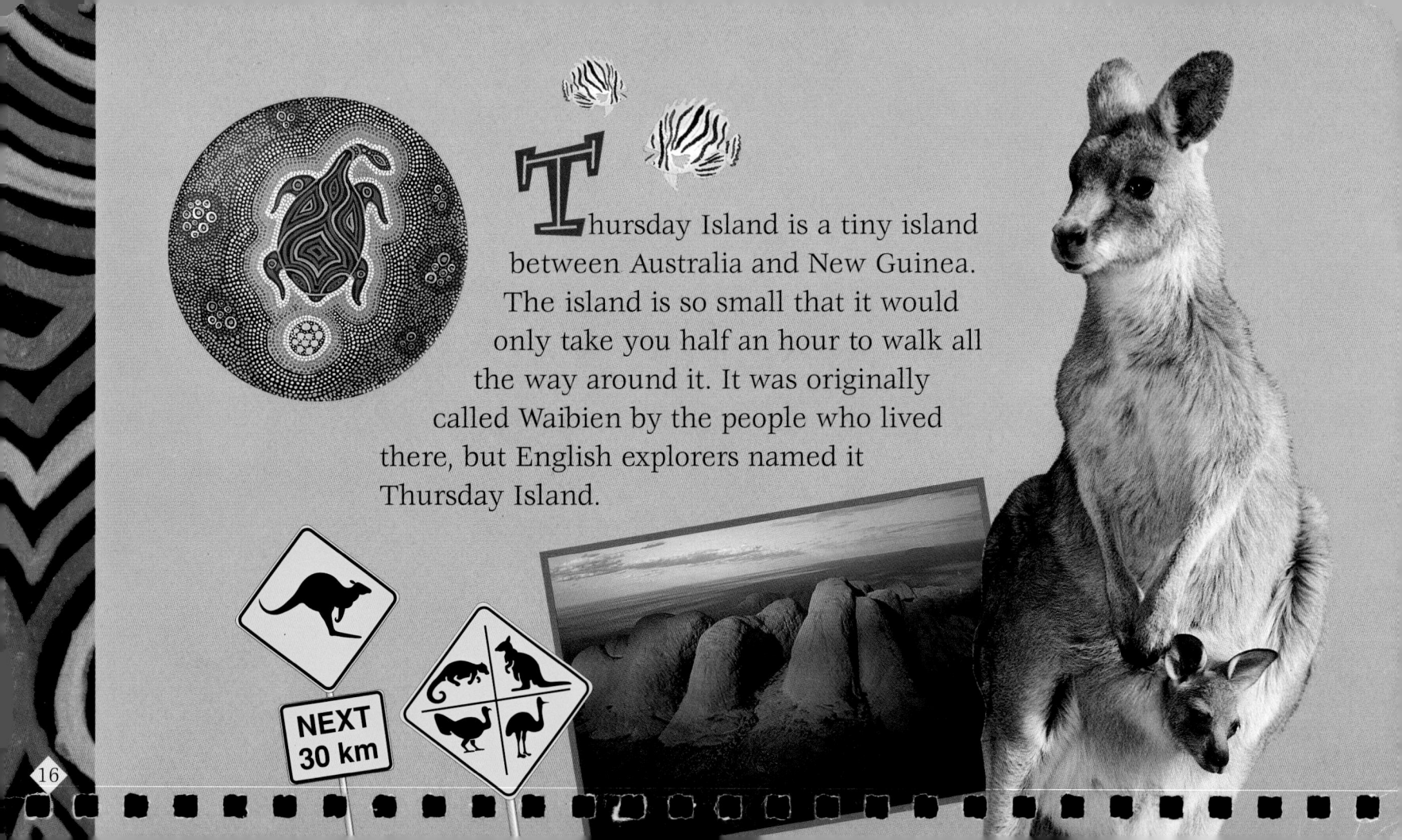

Thursday Island is a tiny island between Australia and New Guinea. The island is so small that it would only take you half an hour to walk all the way around it. It was originally called Waibien by the people who lived there, but English explorers named it Thursday Island.

NEXT
30 km

So many string figures come from the islands in this area—called Torres Strait—that it is practically the string game capital of the world.

Notice that funny mound of dirt behind Trevor in the photo on page 15? That is actually an ant hill. It's not at all unusual to see ant hills this big in Australia.

Trevor Cook   Age: 13

Hometown: Tamwox, Australia

Pets: A dog named Sister

Favorite game: T-Ball

Home: wooden cottage

Most fun he's ever had: "going deer hunting."

PALM TREE

1

Start by looping the string across both of your palms and behind your pinkies and thumbs.

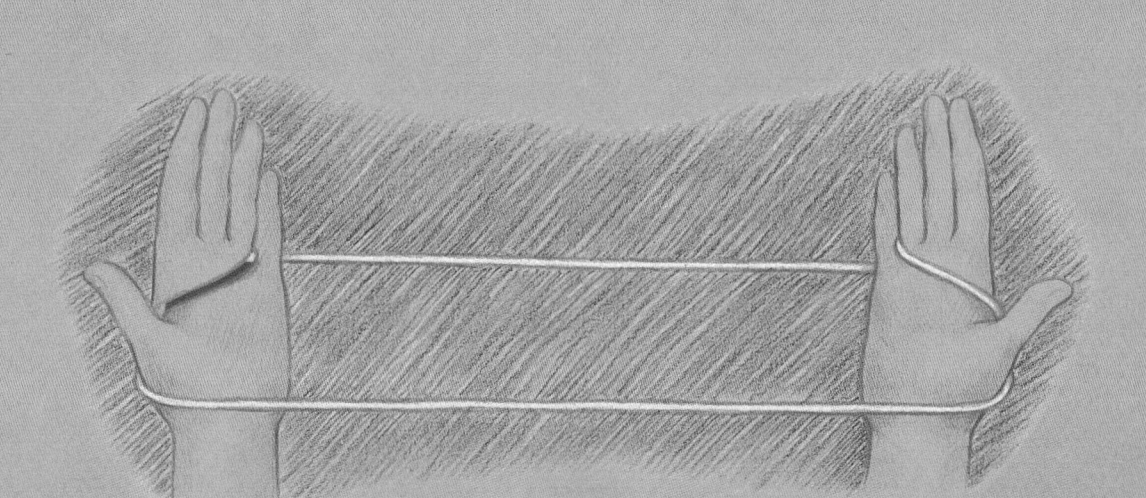

2

Reach across with the first finger
of your right hand and pick up
the string that runs across your
left palm.

Pull your hands apart.

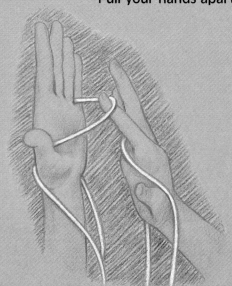

3

Do the same thing with the first
finger of your left hand. Reach across
and pick up the string that runs across
your right palm.

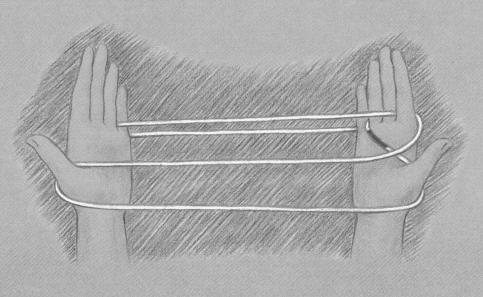

Pull your hands apart and make
sure they match the picture
before you go on.

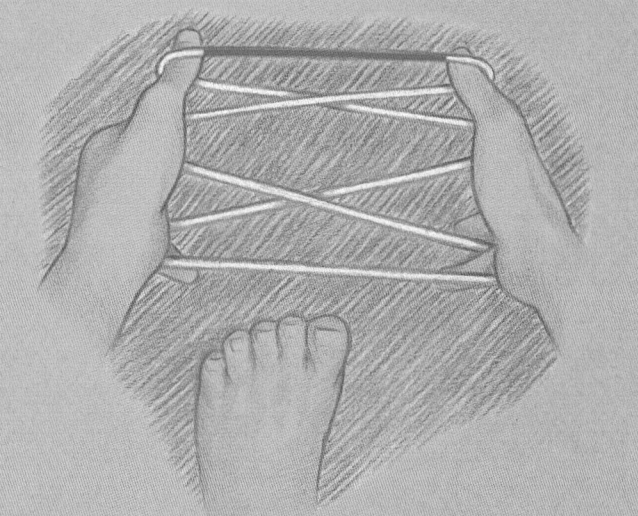

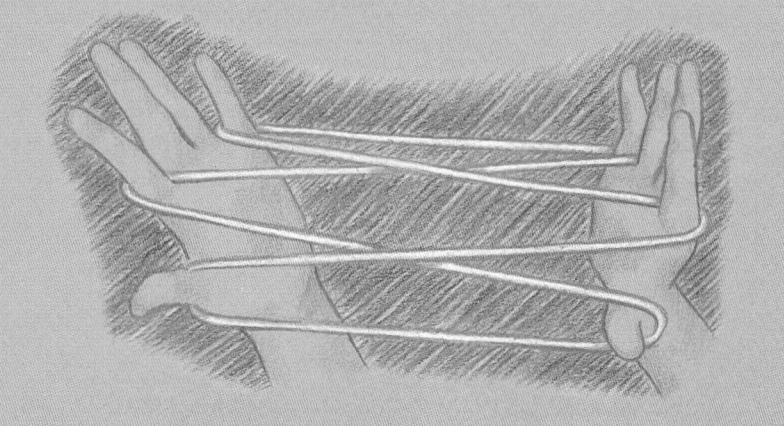

Red marks the string you pick up next.

 Now rest your fingertips straight
down on the floor and find the
string that runs straight across
the outside of your thumbs
(we've marked it in red).

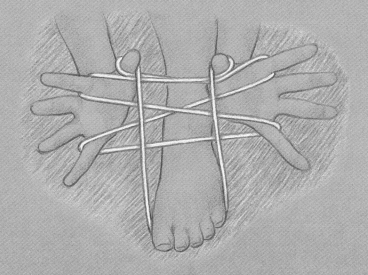

6 Keep your foot (and the string you're stepping on) on the ground and pull your hands up a bit, turning them so your fingertips point away from you. It will look like this from the front:

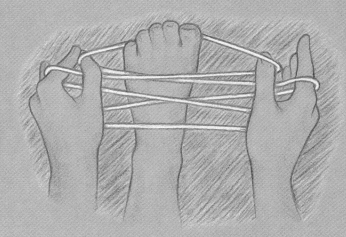

5 Put one foot **under** all the other strings and step on this one.

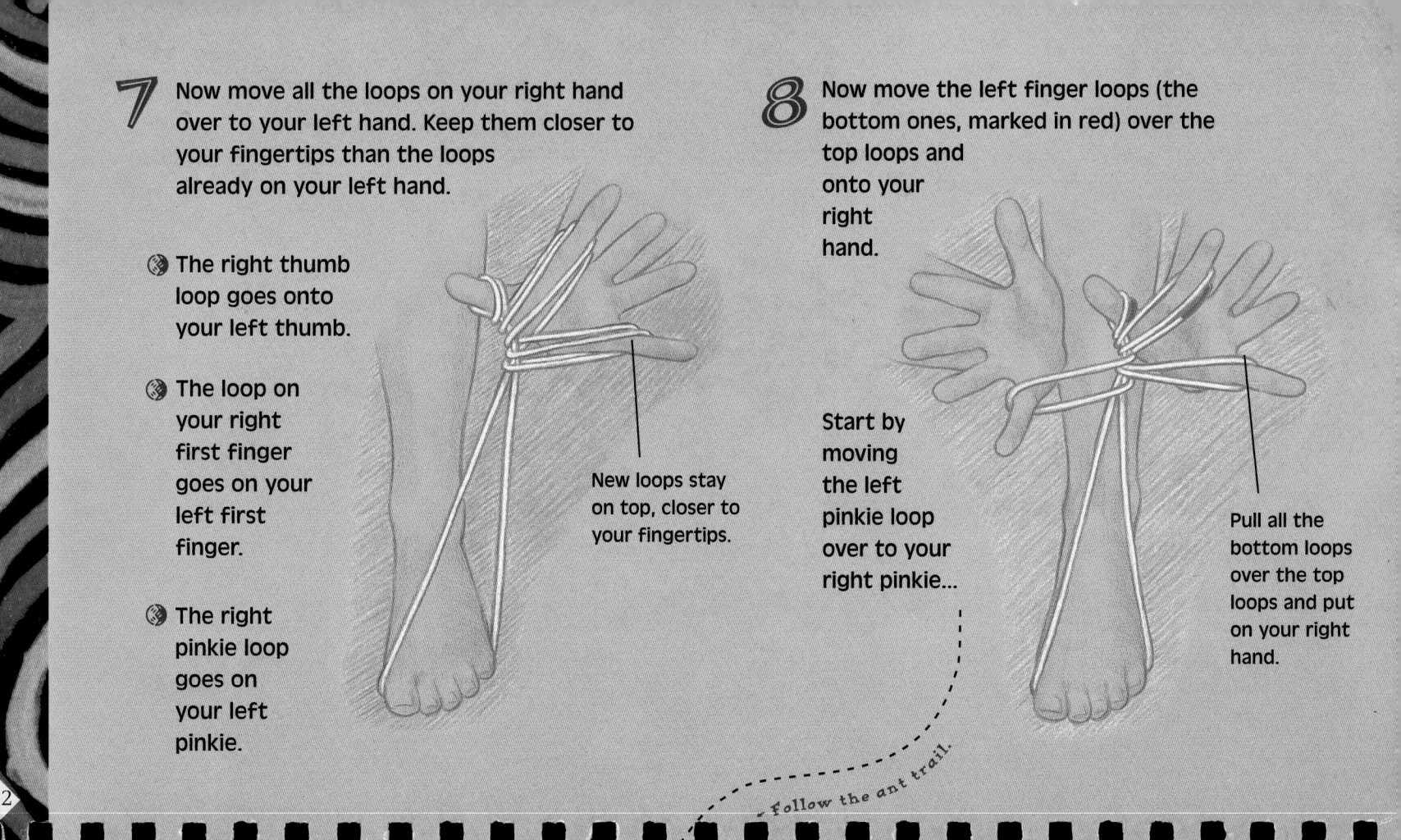

7 Now move all the loops on your right hand over to your left hand. Keep them closer to your fingertips than the loops already on your left hand.

⊛ The right thumb loop goes onto your left thumb.

⊛ The loop on your right first finger goes on your left first finger.

⊛ The right pinkie loop goes on your left pinkie.

New loops stay on top, closer to your fingertips.

8 Now move the left finger loops (the bottom ones, marked in red) over the top loops and onto your right hand.

Start by moving the left pinkie loop over to your right pinkie...

Pull all the bottom loops over the top loops and put on your right hand.

Follow the ant trail.

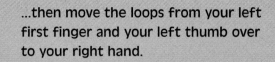

...then move the loops from your left first finger and your left thumb over to your right hand.

9 Pull your hands up a bit more and you've got a palm tree. Wave your hands from side to side to make it sway in the breeze if you want.

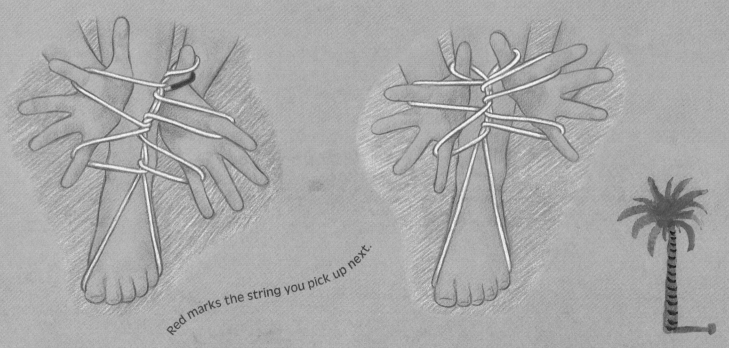

Red marks the string you pick up next.

Banana Tree

The Worm is a string game found all over the world under a lot of different names. In Germany it's a train, in other places it's a mouse. In Ghana (West Africa), where we photographed it, the kids call it the Worm. After you make this figure, pull on one string and the worm will disappear into its hole.

Green Monkey

Ada-Foah is a fishing village on the coast of Ghana. Most of the people there live in mud huts with grass roofs. If you look at the photo of Katuy closely (on page 25), you'll see a very long, very bright boat in the background. This boat was carved out of one VERY big tree trunk. The fishermen stay out in these boats for weeks at a time. The kids in Ada-Foah know a lot of different string games, and it's no surprise that many of them have to do with fishing.

Katuy Adjovu   age: 9

HOMETOWN: Ada-foah, Ghana

PETS: some goats and ducks
(he likes the ducks most)

favorite game: bALL

MOST FUN he's EVER had:
"CHRistmas. We have fireworks."

Trade Beads

SERVAL

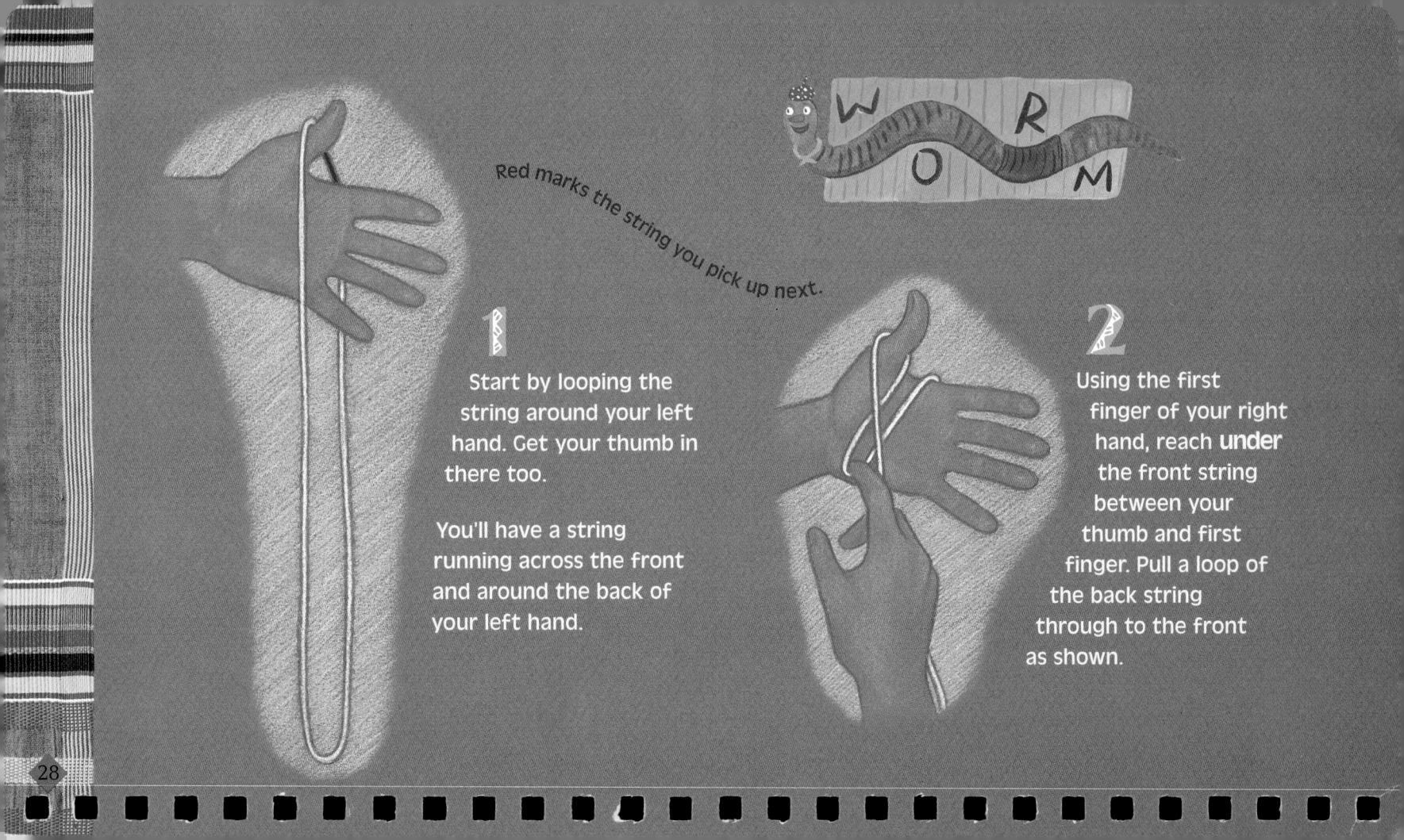

Red marks the string you pick up next.

WORM

1

Start by looping the string around your left hand. Get your thumb in there too.

You'll have a string running across the front and around the back of your left hand.

2

Using the first finger of your right hand, reach **under** the front string between your thumb and first finger. Pull a loop of the back string through to the front as shown.

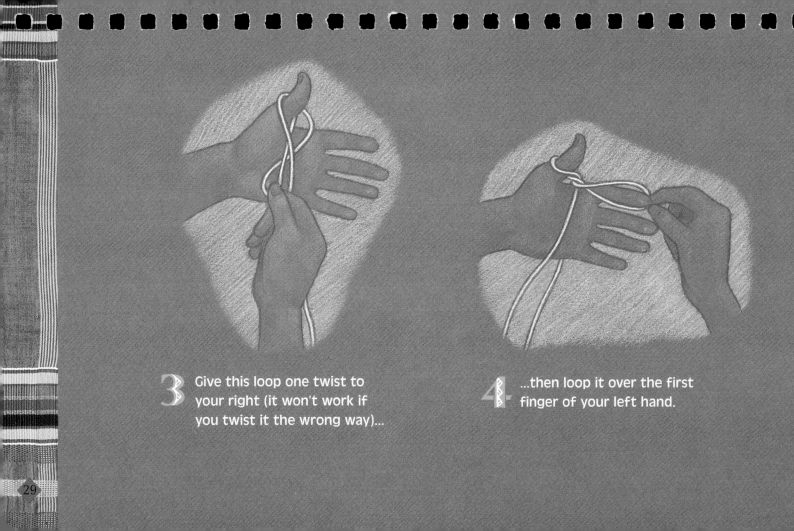

3 Give this loop one twist to your right (it won't work if you twist it the wrong way)...

4 ...then loop it over the first finger of your left hand.

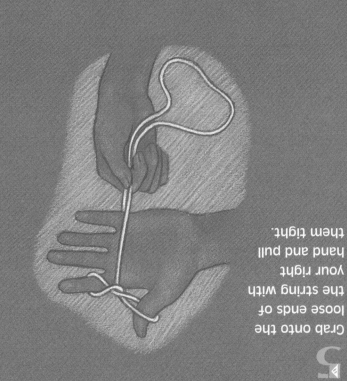

5

Grab onto the loose ends of the string with your right hand and pull them tight.

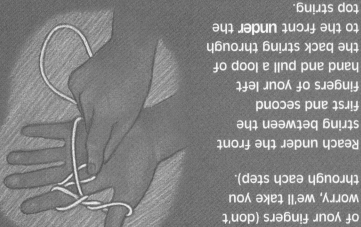

6

Now you're going to do the same thing with the rest of your fingers (don't worry, we'll take you through each step).

Reach under the front string between the first and second fingers of your left hand and pull a loop of the back string through to the front under the top string.

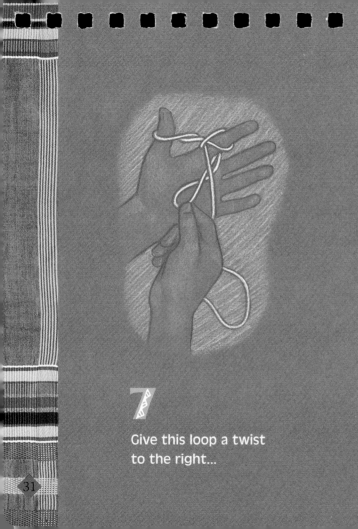

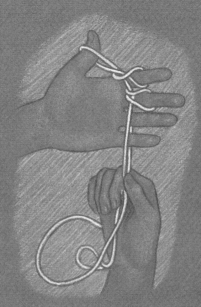

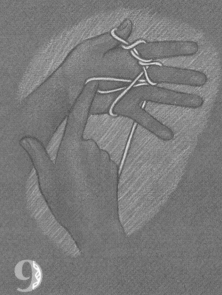

7

Give this loop a twist
to the right...

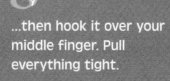

...then hook it over your
middle finger. Pull
everything tight.

9

Reach under the front
string between your
second and third fingers
and pull a loop of the back
string to the front.

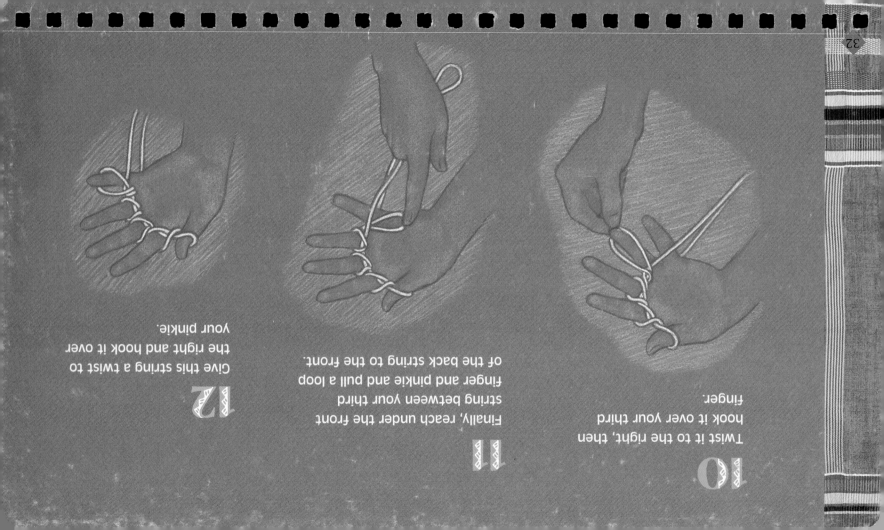

10
Twist it to the right, then hook it over your third finger.

11
Finally, reach under the front string between your third finger and pinkie and pull a loop of the back string to the front.

12
Give this string a twist to the right and hook it over your pinkie.

13

Tug on the loose ends of your string to pull the whole thing tight. This is your worm.

To make the worm disappear into the ground, drop the loop off your thumb, and pull the long front string down.

If your worm didn't disappear like she was supposed to, start over again, this time being extra careful to twist each loop— just once—in the correct direction.

CARRYING WOOD

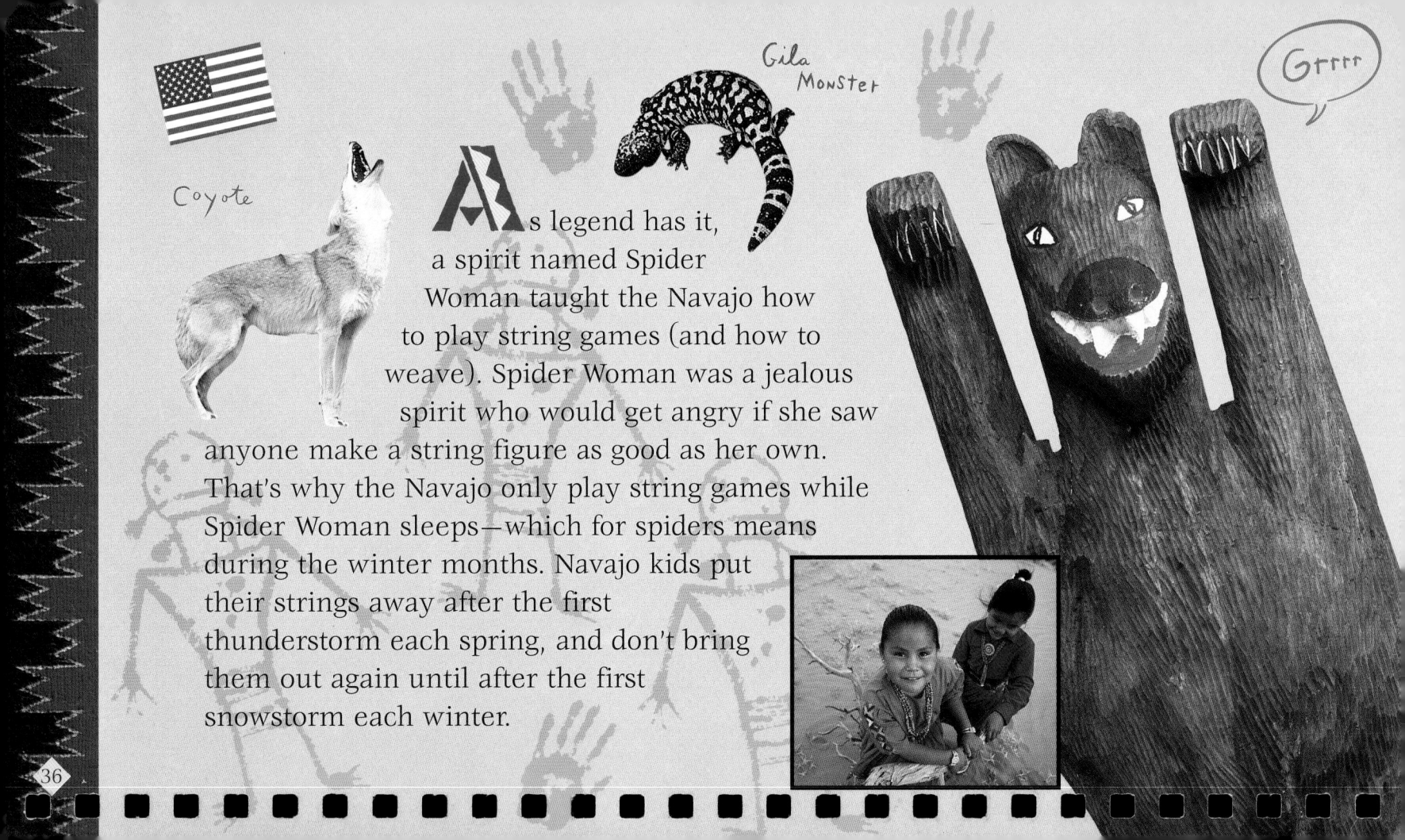

Coyote

Gila Monster

Grrrr

As legend has it, a spirit named Spider Woman taught the Navajo how to play string games (and how to weave). Spider Woman was a jealous spirit who would get angry if she saw anyone make a string figure as good as her own. That's why the Navajo only play string games while Spider Woman sleeps—which for spiders means during the winter months. Navajo kids put their strings away after the first thunderstorm each spring, and don't bring them out again until after the first snowstorm each winter.

Carrying Wood is an old Navajo string figure. When Navajo women used wood fires to keep their hogans warm or to cook over, they usually had to walk pretty far to find their firewood. To make it easier to carry, they bundled all the wood together and supported it from a band strapped around their foreheads.

Mark Minkler   Age: 10
Hometown: Flagstaff, Arizona
Pets: Dog named Sparky
     Cat named Kitty
     Another cat named Kitty
Favorite game: Basketball
Most fun thing he's ever done: "Drive my Dad's car and hunting jackrabbits."

Jackrabbit

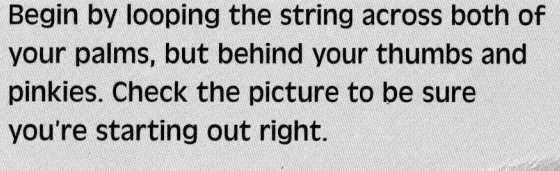

CARRYING WOOD

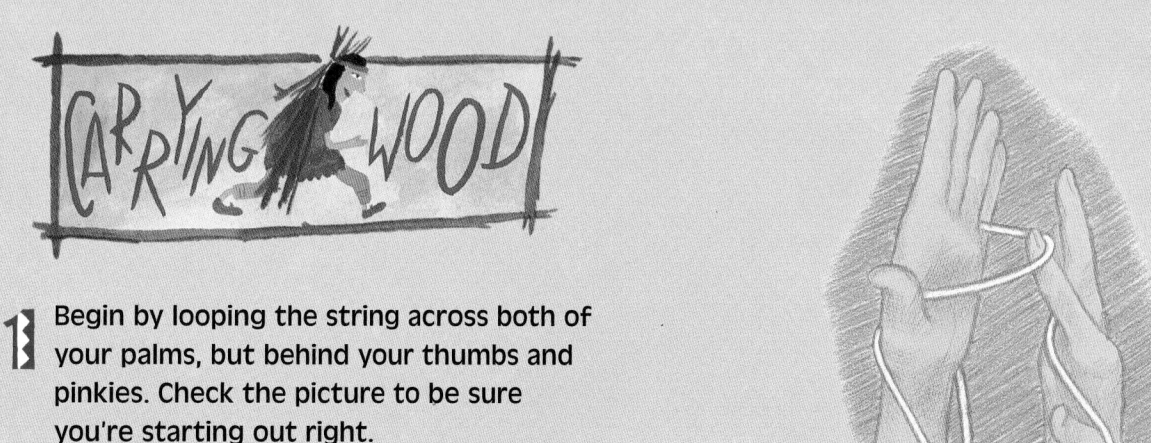

1 Begin by looping the string across both of your palms, but behind your thumbs and pinkies. Check the picture to be sure you're starting out right.

2 Reach across with the first finger of your right hand to pick up the string that runs across your left palm.

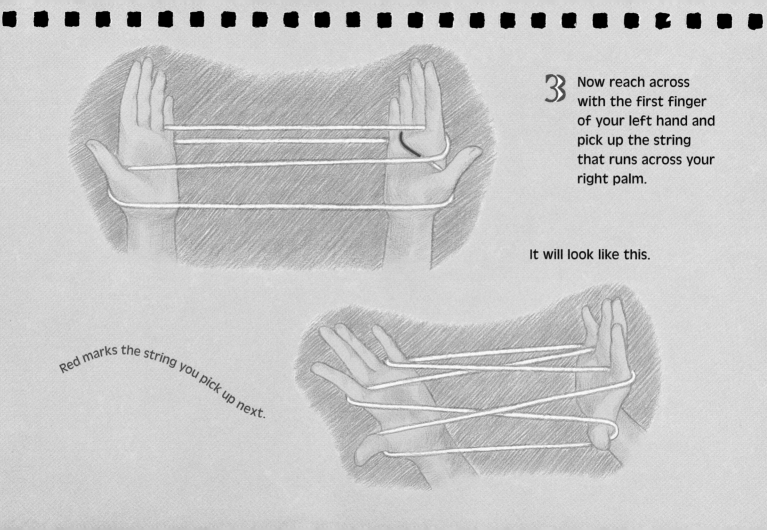

3 Now reach across with the first finger of your left hand and pick up the string that runs across your right palm.

It will look like this.

Red marks the string you pick up next.

4 Pinch your first fingers and thumbs together as shown. (Look at the picture to be sure you've got it right.)

5 Keeping these fingers pinched together, reach over and hook the string we've marked in red from underneath. Don't pinch the string!

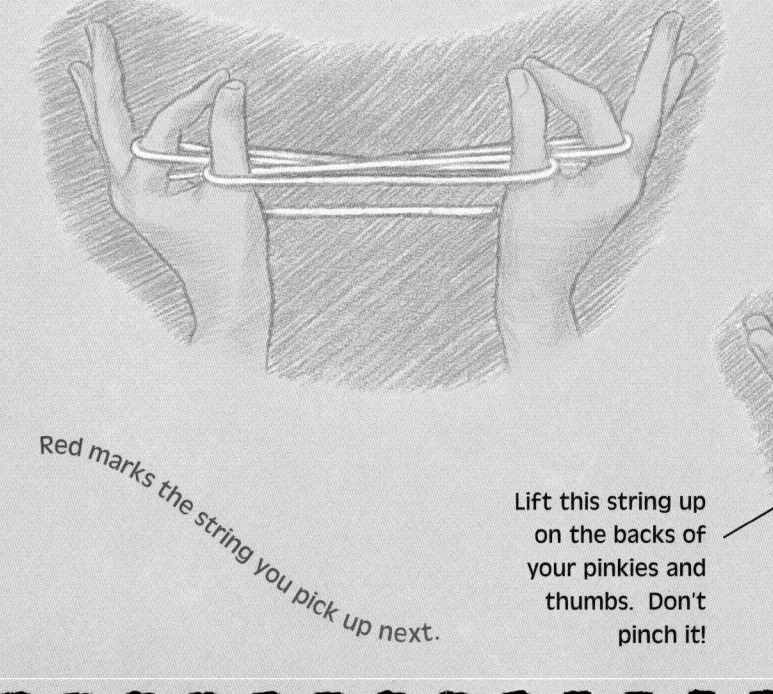

Red marks the string you pick up next.

Lift this string up on the backs of your pinkies and thumbs. Don't pinch it!

6

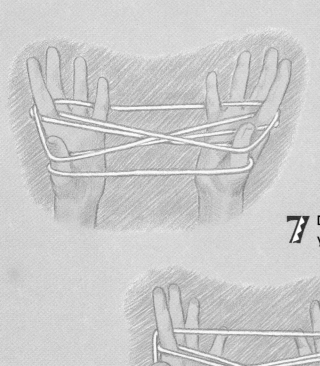

Pull your fingers back to their places, pulling this string along. Spread all your fingers apart and make sure your string looks like the one in the picture.

7 Drop the loops off your pinkies (easy).

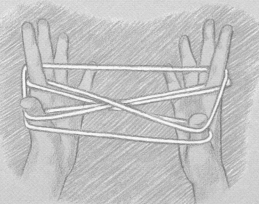

Make sure this string is above the others.

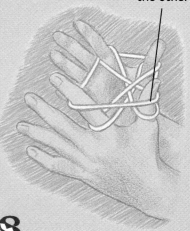

8

Now look at the back of your left hand. Your first finger and thumb should have two loops on them. One will run around both the thumb and first finger. Make sure this one is on top.

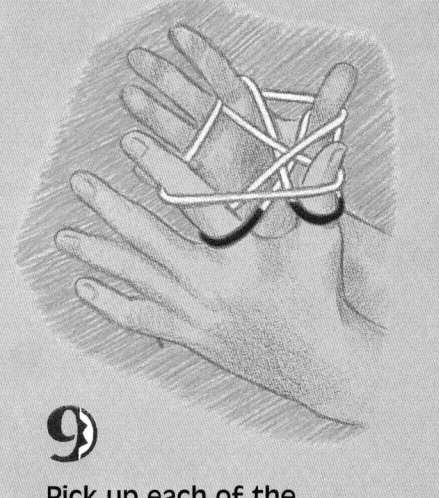

9

Pick up each of the bottom loops (marked in red), pull them up over the top loop and drop them on the palm side of your fingers.

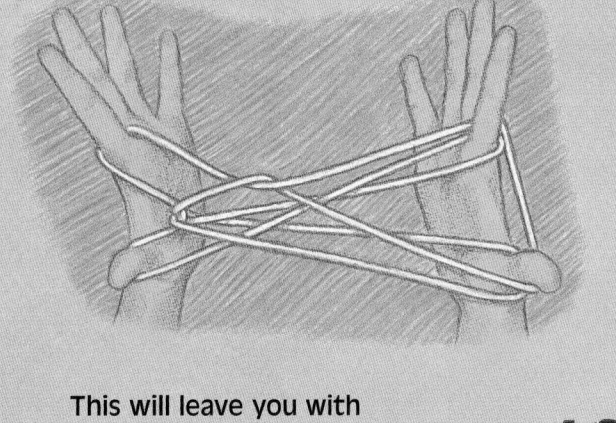

This will leave you with just one loop on the thumb and first finger of your left hand.

Red marks the string you pick up next.

10

Do the same thing with the loops on your right hand. Make sure the loop that runs around your thumb and first finger is on top. Lift the two bottom loops up over the top loops and drop them in front of your fingers.

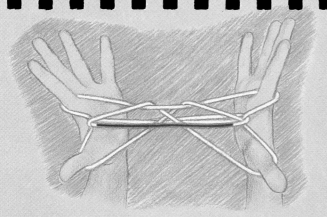

12 Bend your thumbs down and hook them over this string. At the same time, let the thumb loops slip off your thumbs.

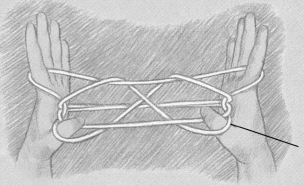

Let thumb loops slip off.

11 Make sure your string looks like this before you go on. Find the string close to you that runs straight between your hands on top of all the other loops. We've marked this string in red.

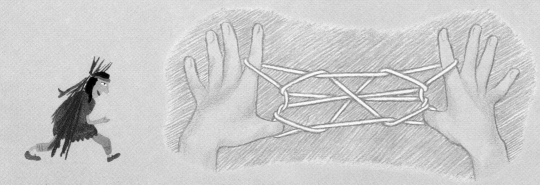

13 Hold your hands up and spread your fingers apart to show the firewood bundled together.

Betl hut
fruit BAT
Irian Jaya
Victoria Crowned Pigeon
sago palm
New Britain
Kingfisher
Bismark Sea
PAPUA New Guinea
PAPUA New Guinea
Yuat River MASK
Fusilier
pig
Port Moresby
AUSTRALIA
Arafura Sea

flying BIRD

Dugong

New Guinea, a big island north of Australia, is famous for its beautiful, exotic birds, so it is natural that the kids there have a string figure showing a bird flying away. They also have string figures that show fish, crocodiles and bananas: all things that are part of their lives.

Bird of Paradise

Stephanie is from the Motua tribe and lives on the coast of New Guinea. She and her neighbors live in houses that are built on stilts out over the water. This helps to cool their houses and keep the bugs out.

STEPHANIE HENDRY Age: 8

HomeTown: Vabukori Village, Papua New Guinea

Pets: A kitten named Annabelle

Favorite game: Skipping

Most fun she's ever had: "Saw a wrestling match. It was fun seeing two very big men wrestle."

Outrigger Canoe

47

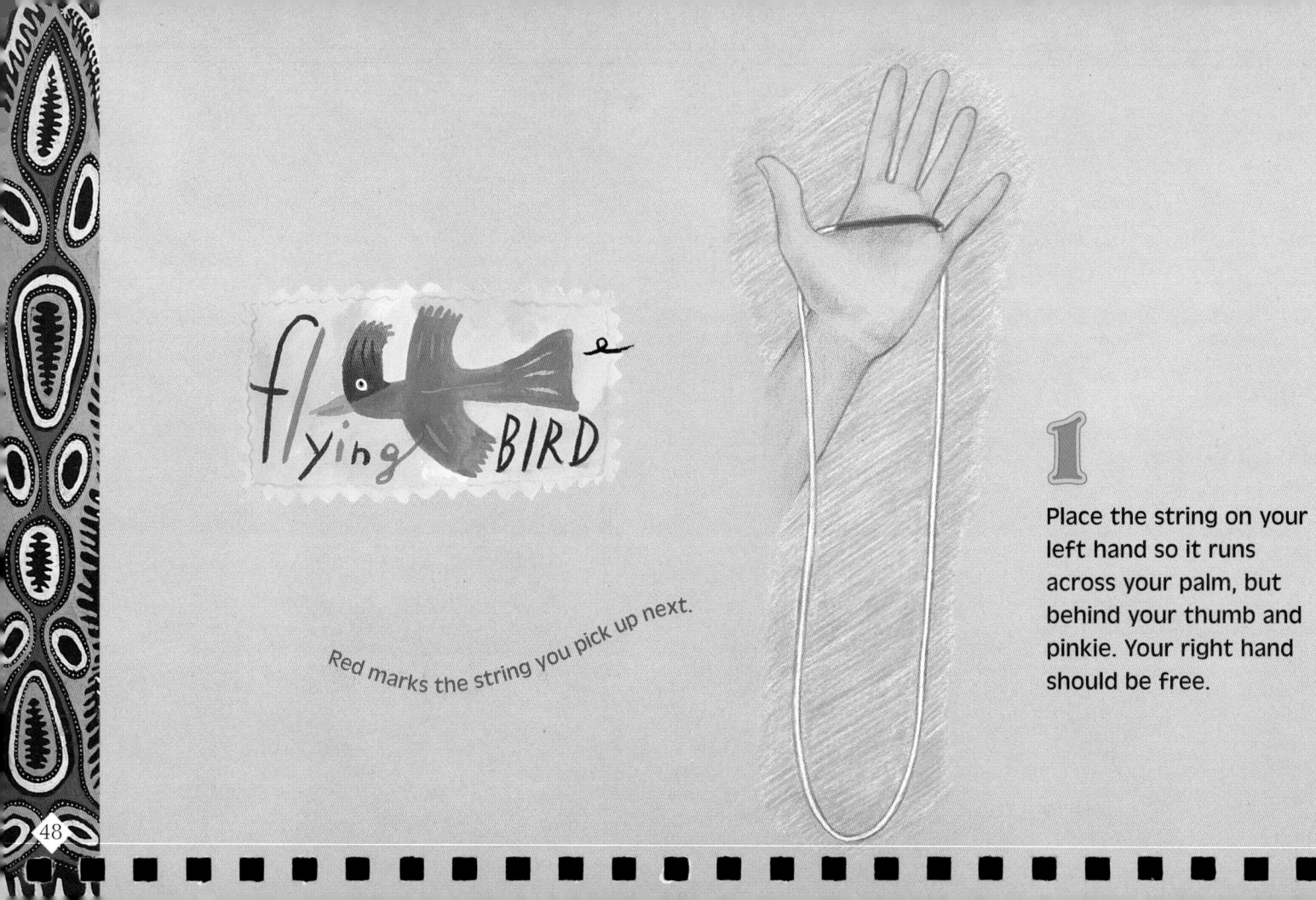

flying **BIRD**

Red marks the string you pick up next.

1

Place the string on your left hand so it runs across your palm, but behind your thumb and pinkie. Your right hand should be free.

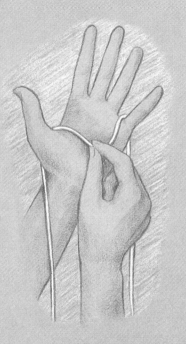

Grab hold of the string that runs across your left palm and pull it all the way down.

The string should look like this:

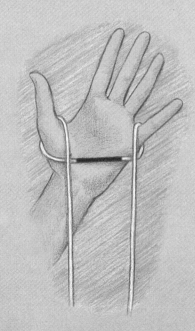

3 Now grab the new string that runs across your palm and pull it all the way down.

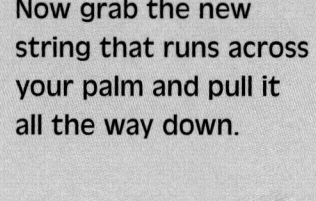

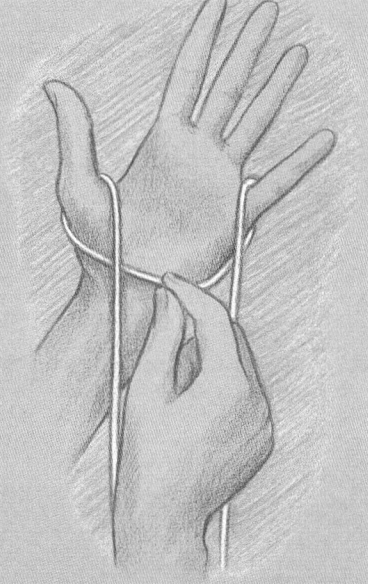

Red marks the string you pick up next.

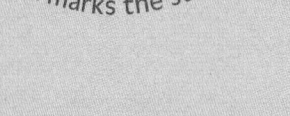

4 Rest the fingers of your right hand against your left palm with your right thumb and pinkie reaching out and under the two hanging strings.

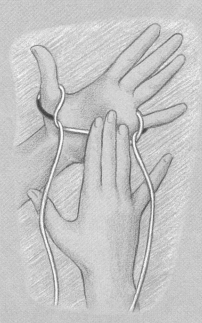

5

Find the loops
that run around the thumb
and pinkie of your left hand
(marked in red).

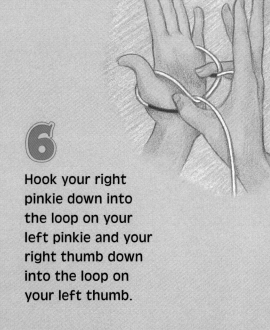

6

Hook your right
pinkie down into
the loop on your
left pinkie and your
right thumb down
into the loop on
your left thumb.

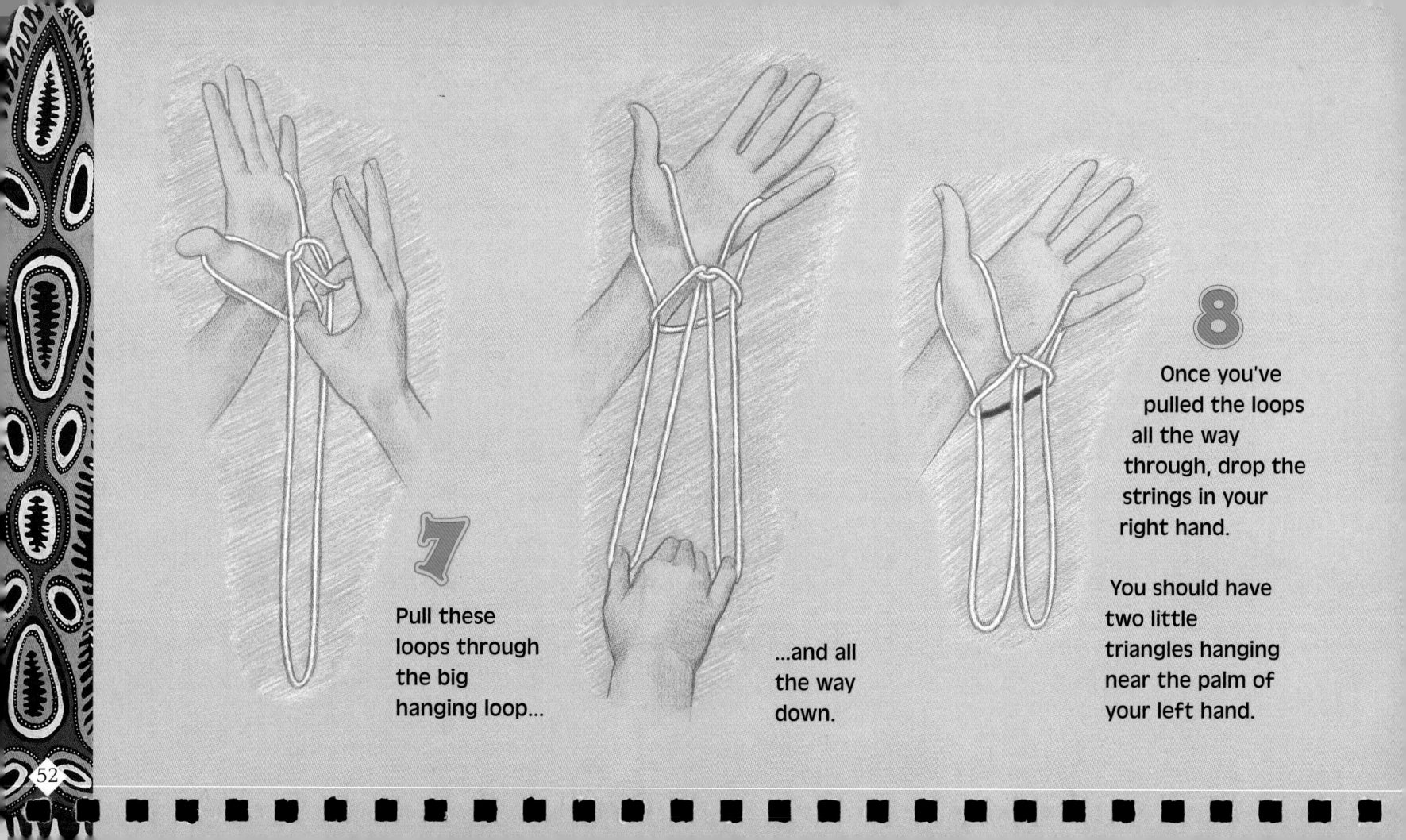

7

Pull these loops through the big hanging loop...

...and all the way down.

8

Once you've pulled the loops all the way through, drop the strings in your right hand.

You should have two little triangles hanging near the palm of your left hand.

9

Hook your right thumb and pinkie behind the bottom string of the two triangles (we've marked these strings in red).

Red marks the string you pick up next.

Pull these strings away from your left hand. This time, don't let go of the strings. You will have made a diamond between your hands.

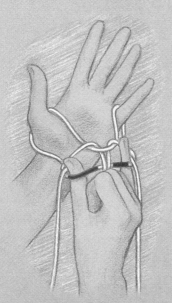

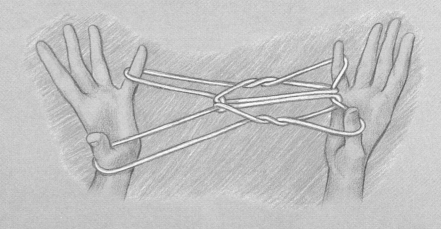

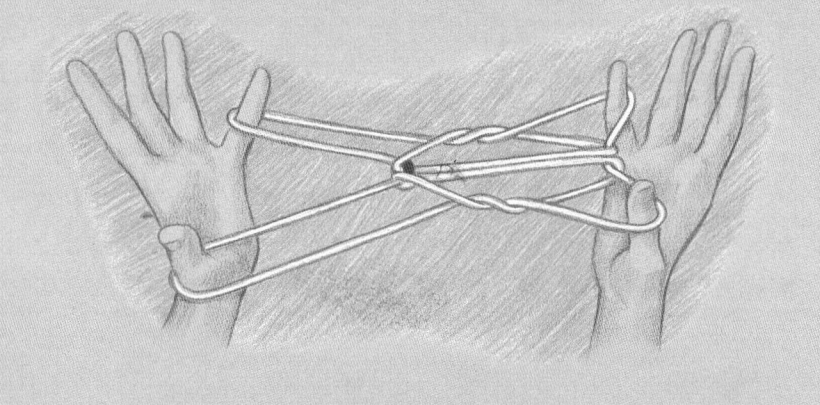

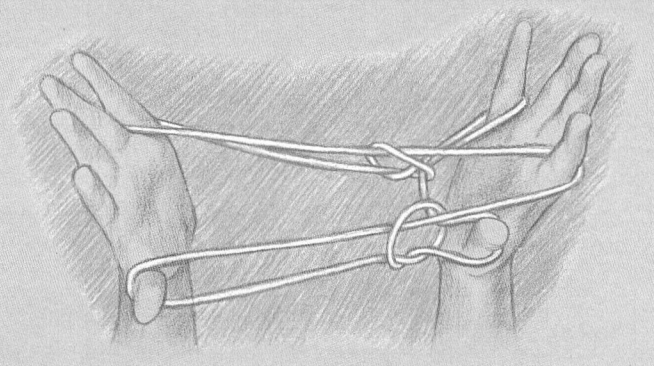

Red marks the string you pick up next.

11 Reach across with the first finger of your right hand and pick up the loop that holds the left point of the diamond (we've marked it in red to make it easy).

12 Pull your hands apart, seesawing your right hand to tighten the two loops into knots.

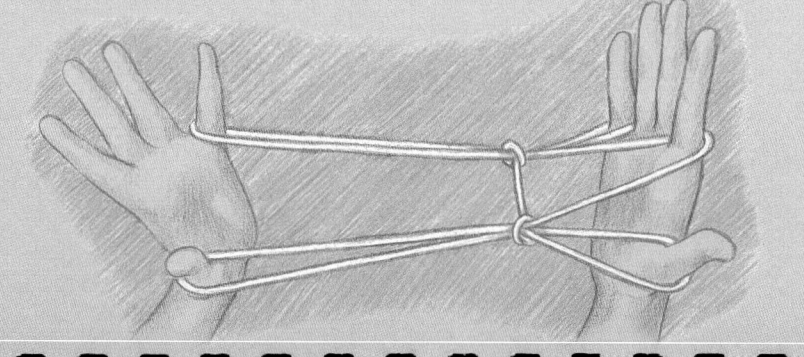

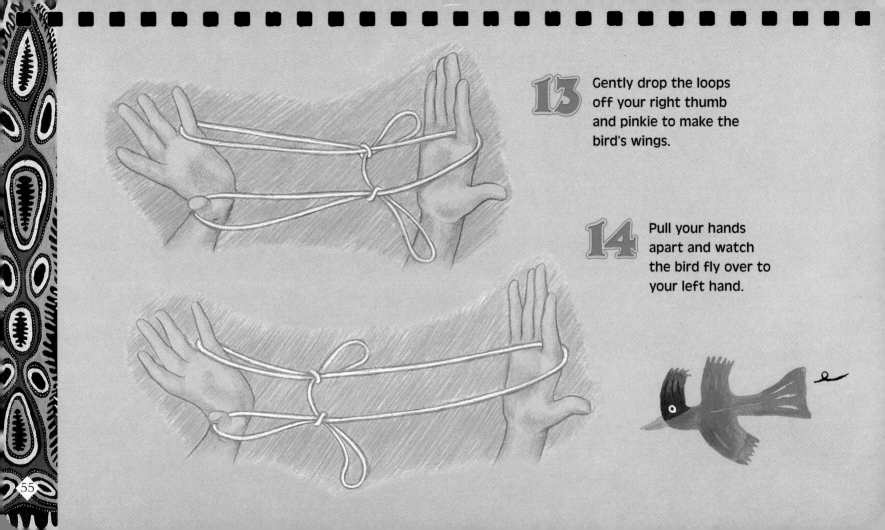

13 Gently drop the loops off your right thumb and pinkie to make the bird's wings.

14 Pull your hands apart and watch the bird fly over to your left hand.

ALASKA
St Lawrence island
Alaska
Canada
U.S.A.
Kayak
RUSSIA
puffin
Bering Strait
St. Lawrence island
Bering Sea
FAirbanks
ALASKA
MT. McKinley
CANADA
Gulf of Alaska

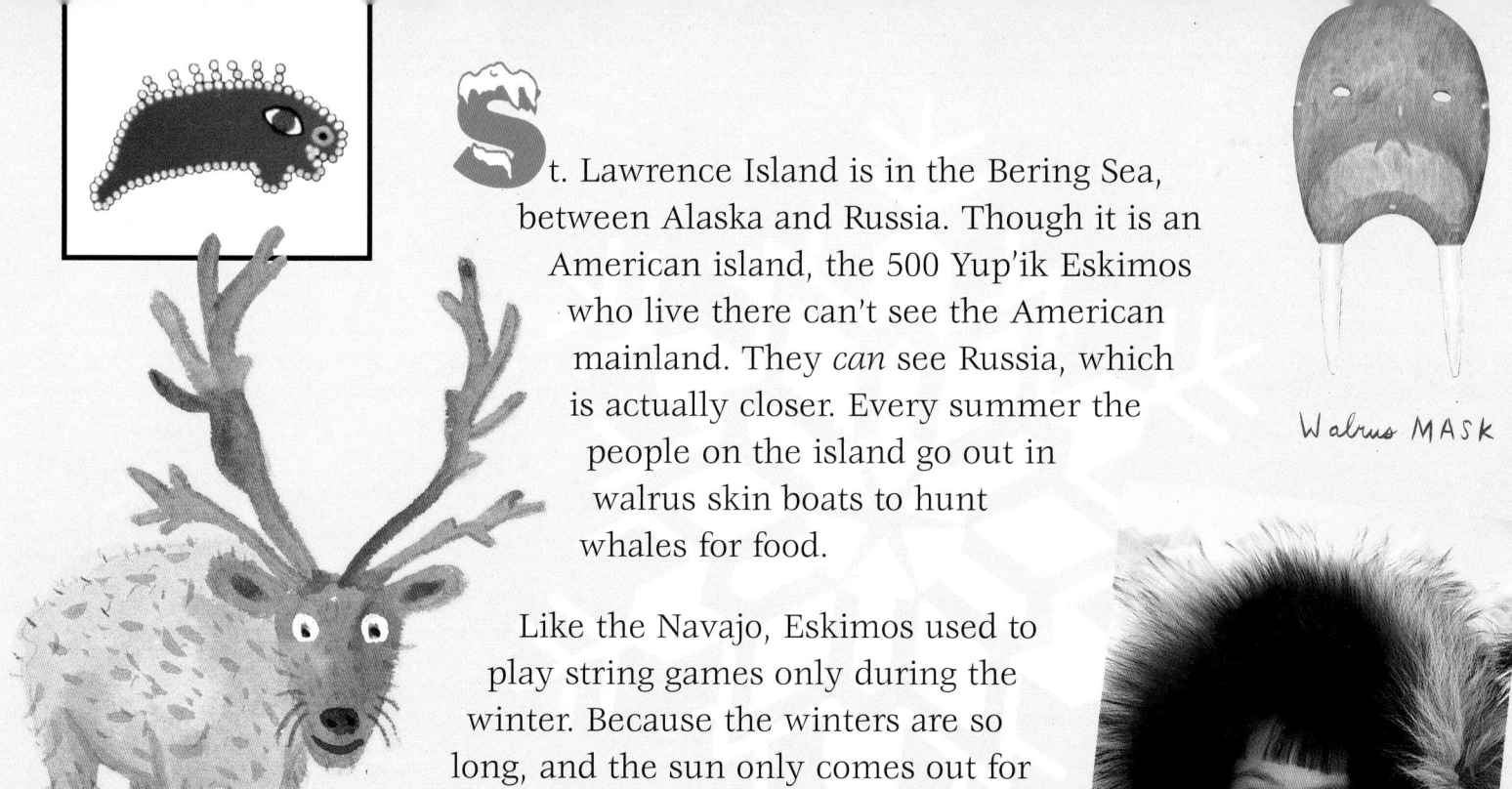

St. Lawrence Island is in the Bering Sea, between Alaska and Russia. Though it is an American island, the 500 Yup'ik Eskimos who live there can't see the American mainland. They *can* see Russia, which is actually closer. Every summer the people on the island go out in walrus skin boats to hunt whales for food.

Like the Navajo, Eskimos used to play string games only during the winter. Because the winters are so long, and the sun only comes out for a few hours a day, they got to be pretty good at string games.

Walrus MASK

Caribou

Uutsie Apatiki   Age: 10

Hometown: Gambell on St. Lawrence Island, United States

Pets: Two dogs, Simba and Lazy

Favorite Game: Basketball

Most amazing thing that ever happened in her town: "The polar bear travelled through it."

The picture of Uutsie on page 57 was taken at around midnight in June. The kids on her island get to play outside late this time of year because it never really gets dark in the summer—that's one good thing about living in Alaska. If you look closely at the picture you'll see a not-so-good thing: Even in June, there's still snow on the ground.

Wolf

59

1 Start by looping the string across both of your palms and behind your pinkies and thumbs.

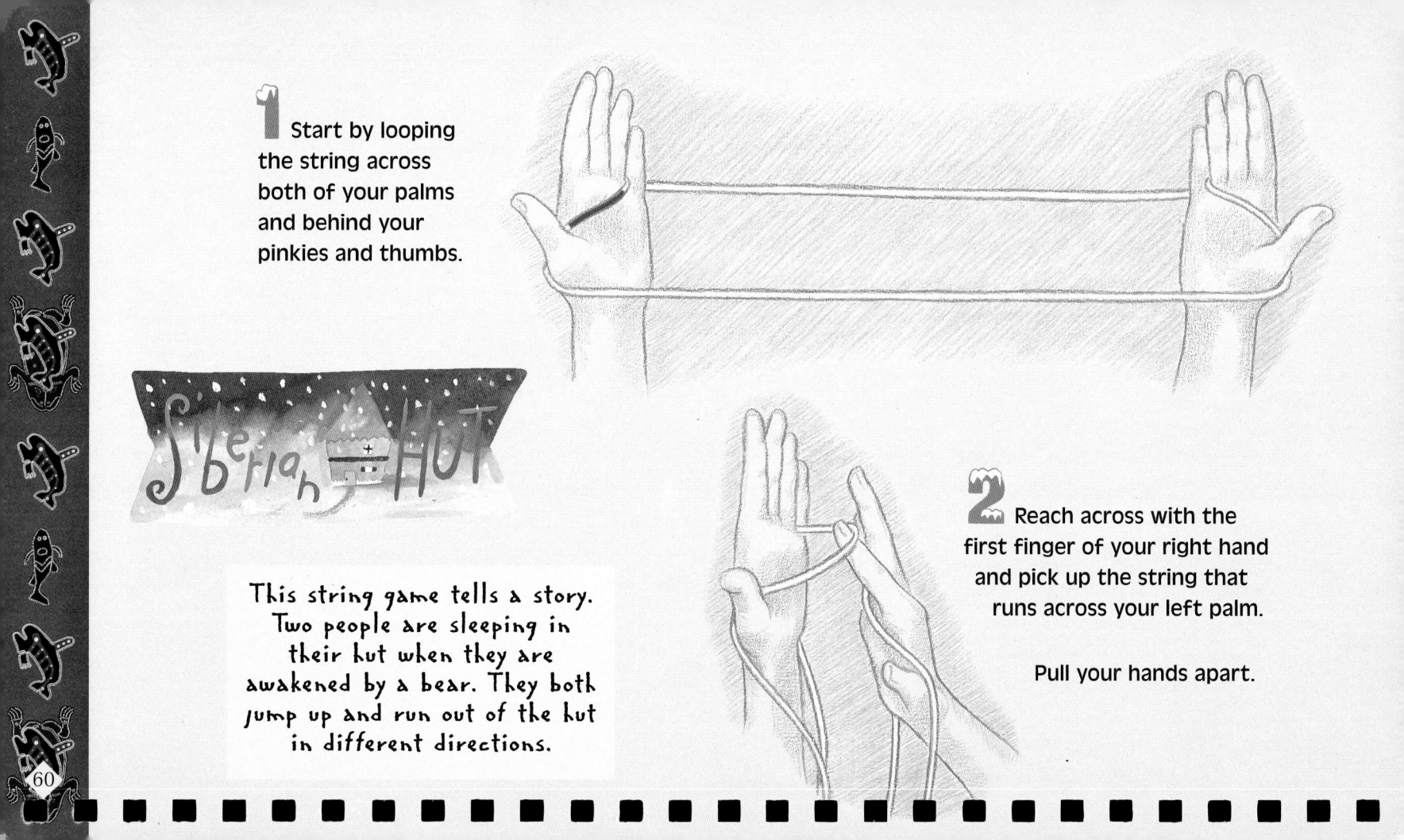

SIBERIAN HUT

This string game tells a story. Two people are sleeping in their hut when they are awakened by a bear. They both jump up and run out of the hut in different directions.

2 Reach across with the first finger of your right hand and pick up the string that runs across your left palm.

Pull your hands apart.

3 Do the same thing with the first finger of your left hand. Reach across and pick up the string that runs across the right palm.

Red marks the string you pick up next.

Pull your hands apart and make sure they match the picture before you go on.

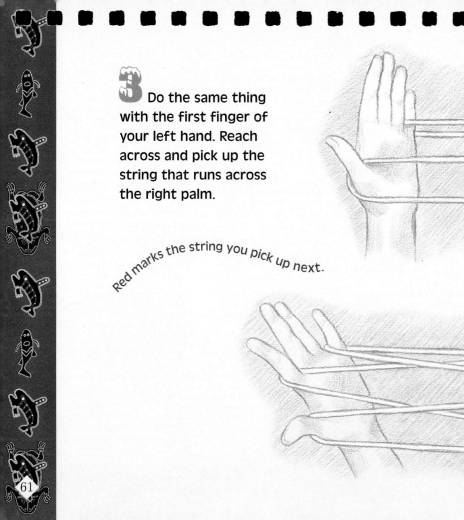

4  Squeeze all your fingers together and turn your palms towards you. Reach your fingers under the string closest to you as shown.

5 Lift the string up off your thumbs and over your fingers so it ends up on the far side of your hands. Turn your hands to face each other again.

Wiggle your hands around a bit so that this string runs below the other string on your pinkies.

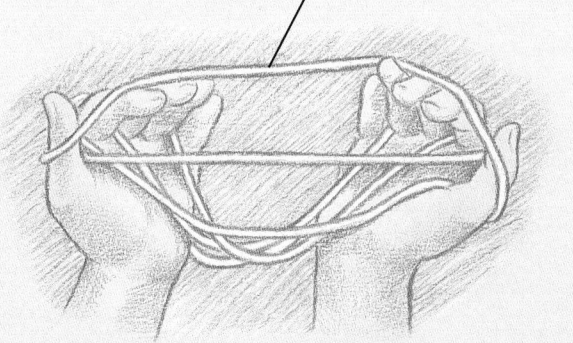

Red marks the string you pick up next.

6 Now look at the two strings closest to you. They make an **X** as they cross each other.

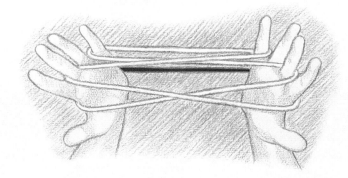

7 Reach your thumbs through the **X**, and pick up the string marked in red (the bottom string that runs around your hands and behind your pinkies).

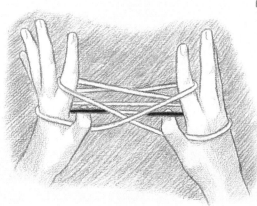

8 Pull this string back through the **X**. Make sure your string looks like this before you go on.

63

9 Now look at the back of your left hand and find the string that runs all the way across. (We've marked it in red.)

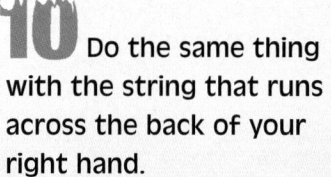

10 Do the same thing with the string that runs across the back of your right hand.

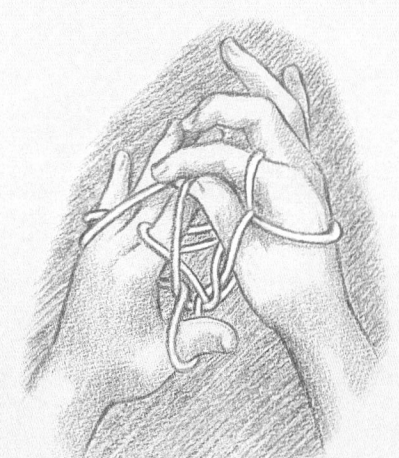

Pick this string up with your right hand, lift it over all your fingers and let it drop in front of your hand.

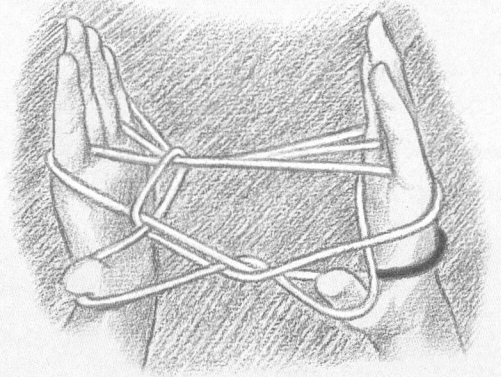

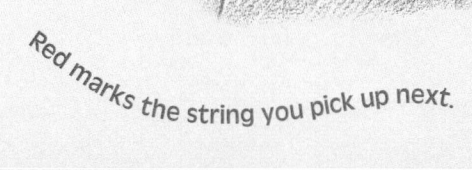

Red marks the string you pick up next.

64

11 Pull your hands apart and hold them out in front of you to show the Siberian Hut.

12 To make the two people inside the hut run away when they hear the bear, drop the loops off your first fingers...

...then slowly pull your hands apart and watch the people run away (this would be a good time to make scary bear noises).

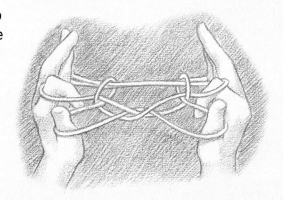

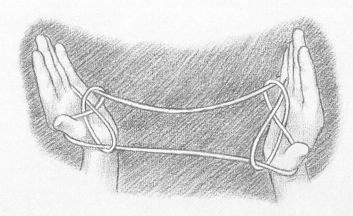

The photo of Colleen and her two brothers was taken near their home at the ruins of an old fortress called Grianan Ailigh. This means "the sun house of Aileach." (Aileach is the name of a princess who once lived in the hilltop fortress.) There are many stories and legends surrounding the fortress, which was built more than 2000 years ago. One story tells of an army of horsemen from a long ago battle, who sleep in a cave near Grianan Ailigh. The sleeping men sit on their horses, waiting to be woken when their help is needed.

Kitty the Donkey

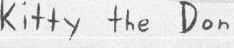

Colleen Quigley Age: 8
(shown on page 67 with her brothers, Dermot and John)

Hometown: Buncrana, Ireland

Favorite game:
Tip the Can

Most fun she's ever had:
"Camping in Bundoran with my Daddy"

String figures are often used to illustrate stories. The Candle Thief—which is also found in Scotland and Germany—tells the story of a man who makes the mistake of stealing a bunch of candles from his neighbor. There is a string game in Papua New Guinea which tells a similar story except that the man steals his neighbor's pigs instead of candles, and while the candle thief gets caught in the end, the pig thief gets away.

Irish Setter

Hedgehog

CANDLE THIEF

This string game tells the story of a man who steals some candles, and then gets caught and sent to jail.

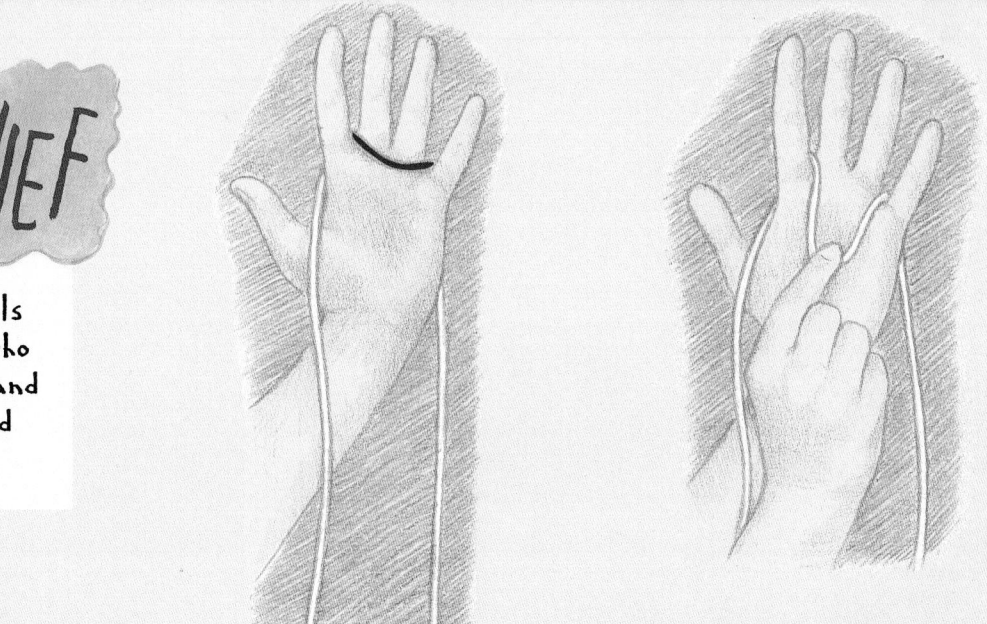

1 Start by looping the string on your left hand exactly as shown: behind your first finger, in front of your two middle fingers and behind your pinkie.

2 With your right hand, pick up the string that runs across your two middle fingers and pull it all the way down.

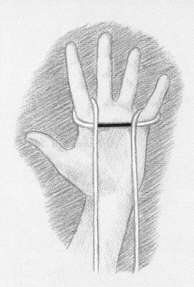

3 Pick up the section of
string that we've marked
in red (it runs across
your palm)...

...and lift it over and behind
your two middle fingers.

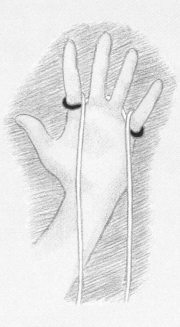

Pull down on the long
strings that hang in front
of your palm to tighten
everything.

Red marks the string you pick up next.

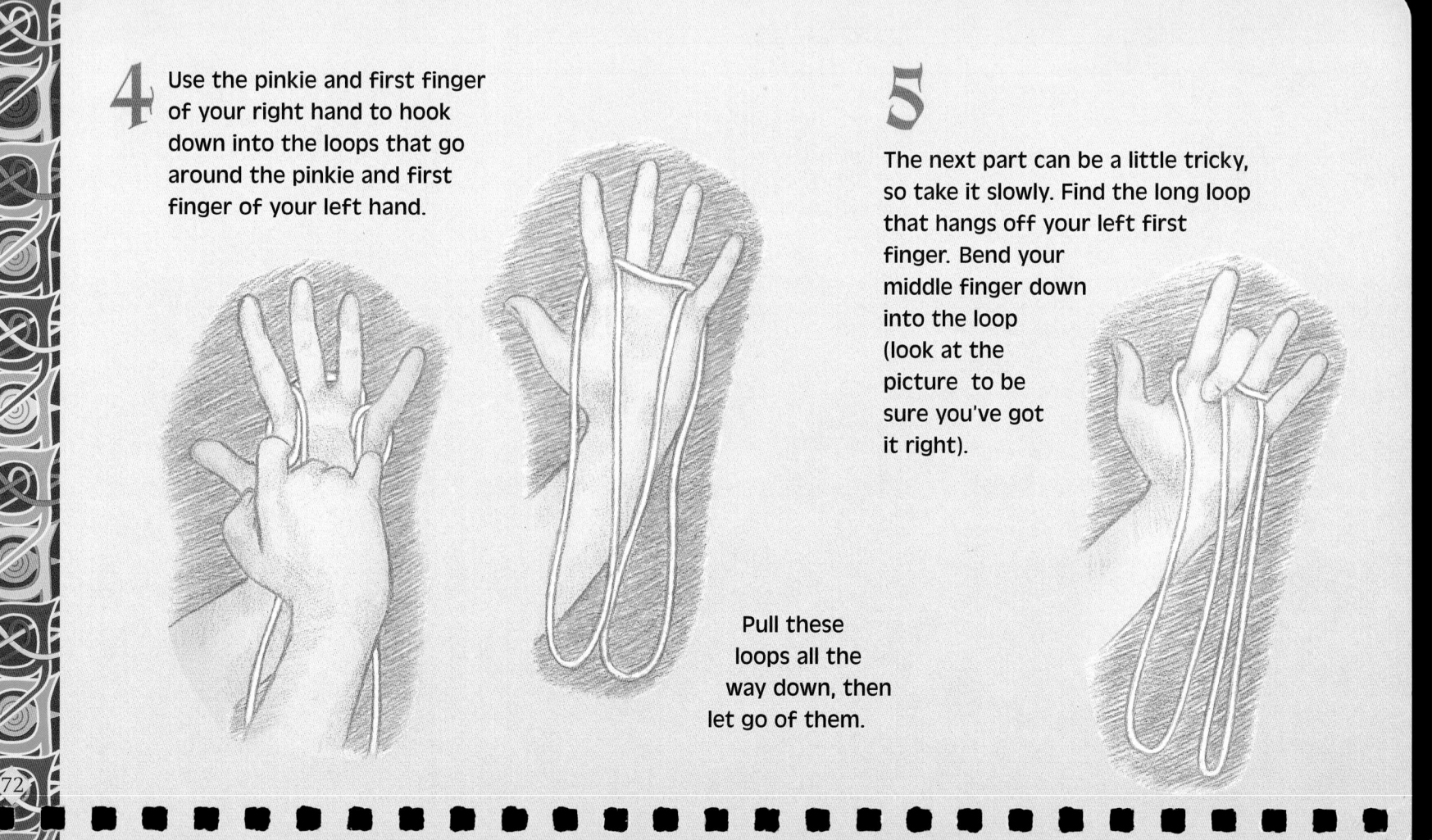

4 Use the pinkie and first finger of your right hand to hook down into the loops that go around the pinkie and first finger of your left hand.

5 The next part can be a little tricky, so take it slowly. Find the long loop that hangs off your left first finger. Bend your middle finger down into the loop (look at the picture to be sure you've got it right).

Pull these loops all the way down, then let go of them.

72

Now pull the loop around to the back of your hand. When you do this, one side of the loop will pass on either side of your bent finger (check out the picture).

Make sure that there is one piece of string on each side of this finger.

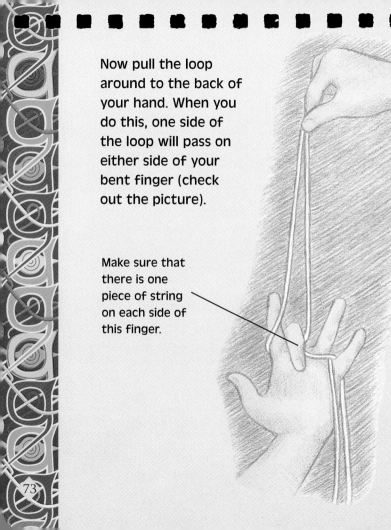

It will look like this from behind.

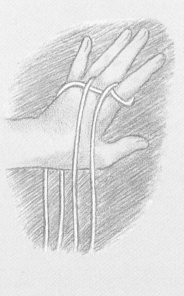

6

Now find the long loop that hangs off your pinkie.

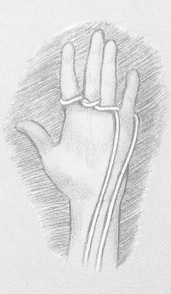

73

7

Bend your third finger (next to your pinkie) down into this loop, then pull the loop to the back of your hand over this finger.

This time, make sure that one string of the loop passes on either side of your bent finger (one side will go between your third and middle finger, and one will go between your third finger and pinkie).

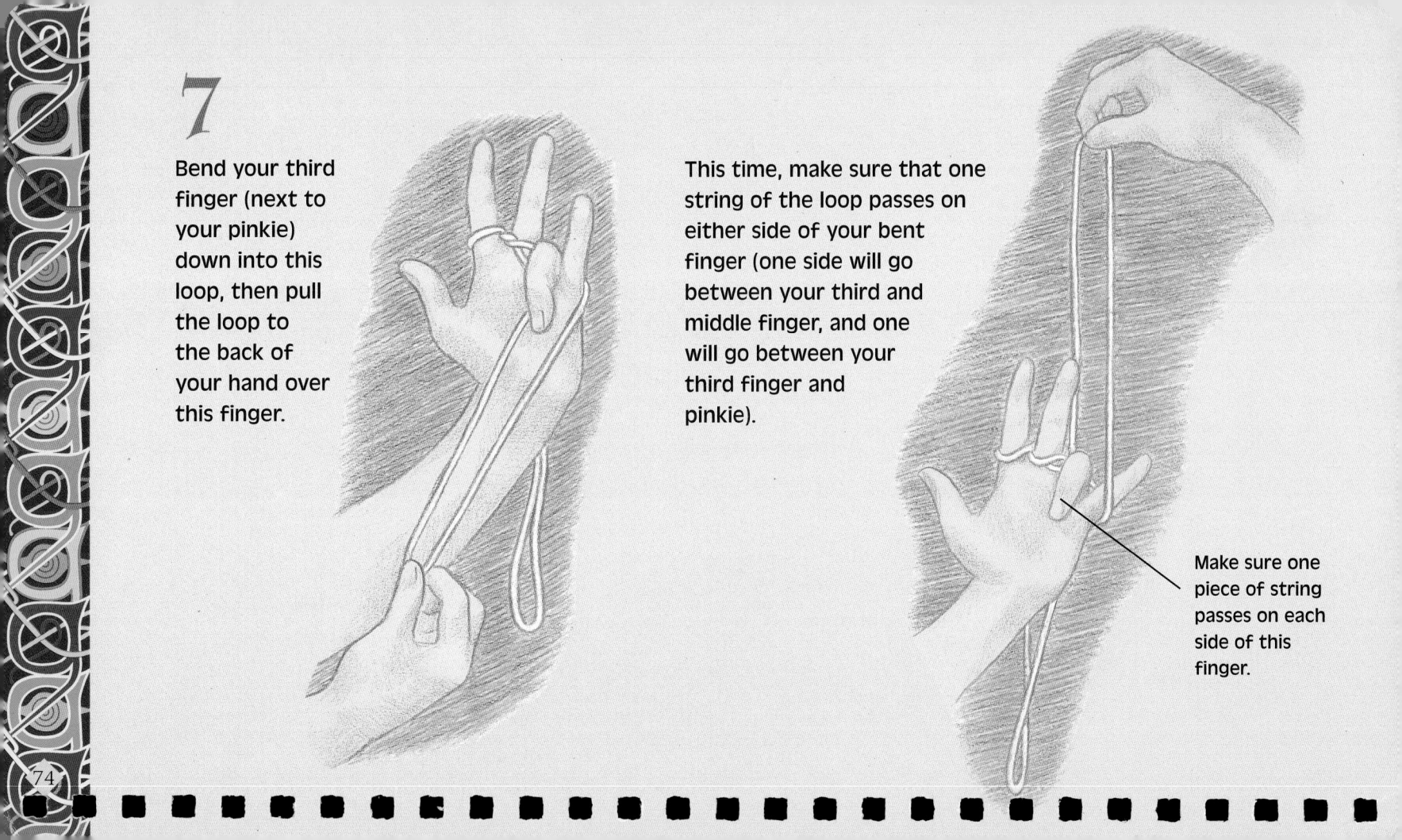

Make sure one piece of string passes on each side of this finger.

8

Turn your hand over and gather all the loose ends together in your right hand.

Red marks the string you pick up next.

9

Tuck these strings under the loop that runs across the two middle fingers of your left hand. Pull them all the way through.

Make sure your string looks just like this before you go on.

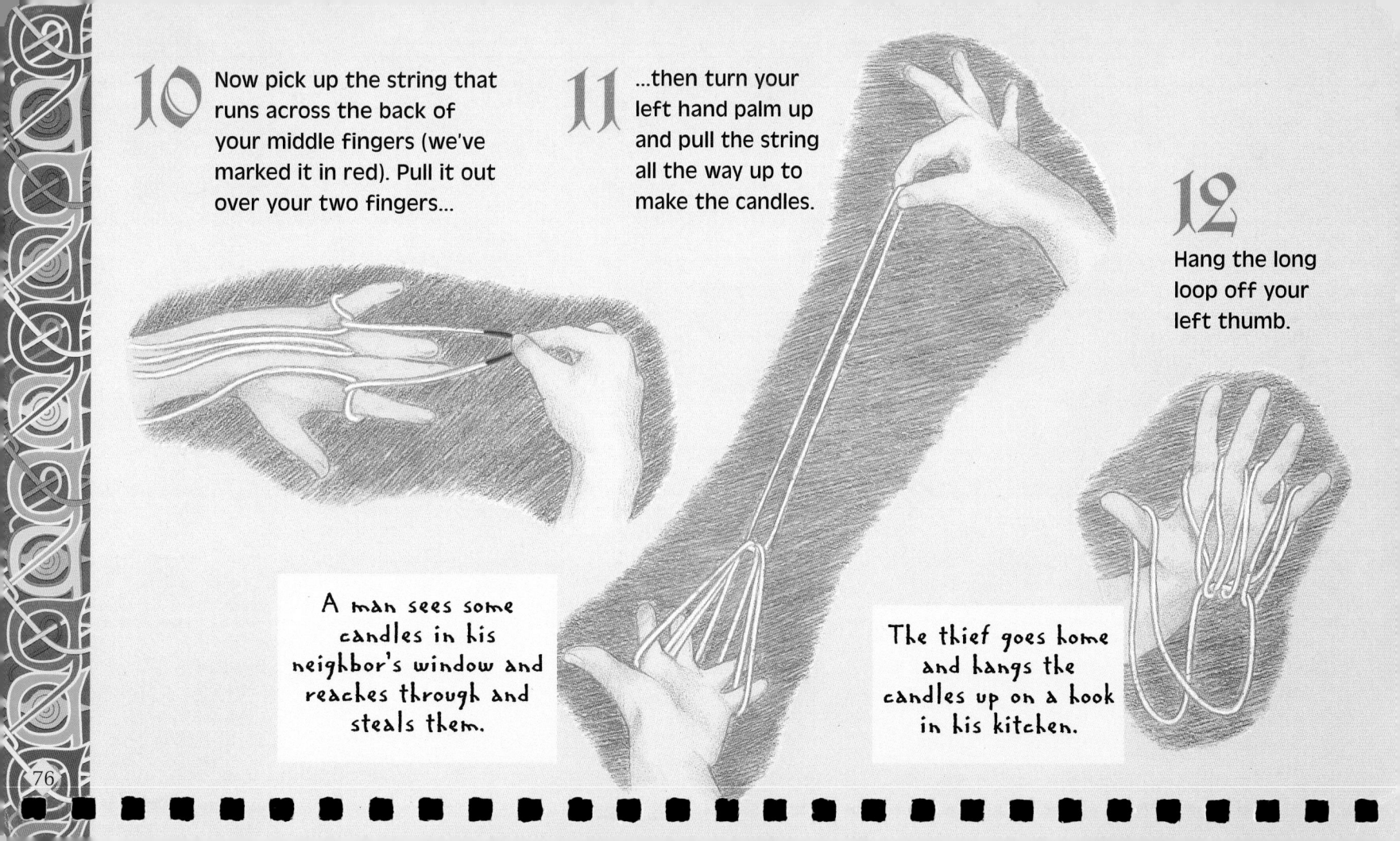

10 Now pick up the string that runs across the back of your middle fingers (we've marked it in red). Pull it out over your two fingers...

11 ...then turn your left hand palm up and pull the string all the way up to make the candles.

12 Hang the long loop off your left thumb.

A man sees some candles in his neighbor's window and reaches through and steals them.

The thief goes home and hangs the candles up on a hook in his kitchen.

13

Squeeze the fingers of your left hand together and look at the back of this hand again.

Using the first and middle fingers of your right hand, pick up the loops running across your middle fingers.

Pull these loops out off your left fingers and around to the front of your left hand...

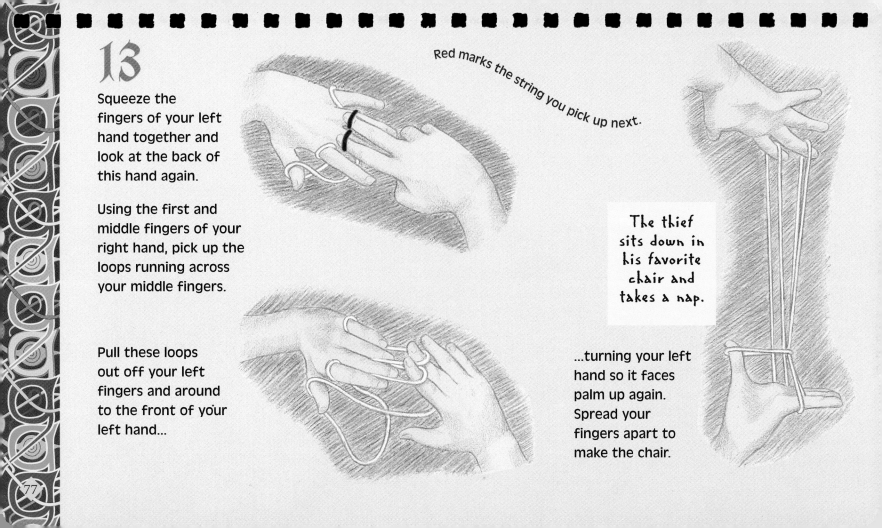

Red marks the string you pick up next.

The thief sits down in his favorite chair and takes a nap.

...turning your left hand so it faces palm up again. Spread your fingers apart to make the chair.

14 Drop the string off your left thumb to make the scissors. Move the fingers on your right hand together and apart to make the scissors cut.

(This will work better if the loops on your right hand are close to the ends of your fingers).

When he wakes up, it's getting dark. He finds his scissors, cuts a candle off the bundle and lights it.

15 Now drop the loop from your left pinkie and pull your hands apart to make the policeman's night stick.

A policeman walks by, sees the light and raps on the thief's door with his night stick.

16 Drop the loop off your right middle finger, then open up the loop on your first finger...

...and put your right hand all the way through this loop.

17 Put your left hand all the way through the loop in your left hand and pull your hands apart. These are the handcuffs.

The policeman handcuffs the thief, and takes him down to the station.

CREDITS PAGE

Cover art and watercolor illustrations by Jessie Hartland, unless otherwise indicated. All instructional drawings by Sara Boore.

Inside front cover: weaving from Ghana, courtesy of Folk Art International, photo by Peter Fox. Page 1: photo of Kofi Teye Mensah by Crispin Hughes. Copyright page 2: bear sculpture by Robin Willeto, 1991 (cottonwood stained with commercial rug dye, 49" x 16" x 7"), photo courtesy of Chuck & Jan Rosenak. Page 4: photo of Katuy Adjovu & Mercy Katuy by Crispin Hughes. Page 5: left, Pygmy woman playing string games, ©Survival International; right, photo of Mark Minkler by John Running. Page 7: photo of Dionesia by John Maier. Page 8: right, hyacinthine macaw (Anodorhynchus hyacinthinus) Animals, Animals/© 1989 Jim Tuten; center, tapir (Tapirella bairdii) Animals, Animals/©C.C. Lockwood; left, nanduti lace from the collection of Gracie Larson, photo by Peter Fox. Page 9: from right, Paraguayen flag; photo of foot on soccer ball by John Maier; photo of Dionesia by John Maier; handwriting by Rachel Gale Jacobson; embroidered bird, collection of Marilyn Green, photo by Peter Fox; nanduti lace, ©1989 Haroldo & Flavia de Faria Castro/FPG International Corp. Page 15: photo of Trevor Cook by Gary Johnston. Page 16: clockwise from left, detail of ceramic plate by Ronald Williams, collection of Heidi Lewis, photo by Peter Fox; ceramic plate,

collection of Heidi Lewis, painted by Ronald Williams, photo by Peter Fox; Australian flag; grey kangaroo with joey (Macrous giganteus), Animals, Animals/©Fritz Prenzel; the Olgas in N. Territory, Australia, ©Jake Rajs/The Image Bank. Page 17: handwriting by Teresa Roberts; E. Australian bark painting, Jocelyn Clapp/Bettmann Archives. Page 25: photo of Katuy Adjovu by Crispin Hughes. Page 26: clockwise from left, cloth border courtesy of Folk Art International, photo by Peter Fox; Benin masks, "The Lovers", ©Carol Beckwith & Angela Fisher/Robert Estall photo agency; gold jewelry worn as insignia by senior officials of the court of the Ashanti kings, 18–19th century, Werner Forman Archive, British Museum, London, ©Werner Forman/Art Resource, N.Y.; drawing of straw hut in Ghana by Kong Lu; Ghanaian flag. Page 27: from left, Shai Dipo, ©Carol Beckwith & Angela Fisher/Robert Estall photo agency; photo of beads by Peter Fox; handwriting by Mark Phillips; serval (Felis serval, endangered species), ©1990 Gail Shumway/FPG International Corporation. Page 35: photo of Mark Minkler by John Running. Page 36: from left, detail of Navajo rug woven by T.P. Hubbles, ©1975 John Running; United States flag; coyote (Canis latrans), ©1993 Gail Shumway/FPG International Corp.; gila monster (Heloderma suspectum), Animals, Animals/©Zig. Leszczynski; Navajo girls photo ©Paul Grebliunas/Tony Stone Images; bear sculpture, see page 2. Page 37: from left, Navajo dolls, collection of Marilyn Green, photo by Peter Fox; handwriting by Sonia Rosner; sheepherding in Canyon de Chelly, AZ, photo ©John Running. Page 45: photo of Stephanie Hendry by Gary Johnston. Page 46: from left, border photo by Peter Fox; dugong drawing by Kong Lu; young

boys at sing-sing, ©Schafer & Hill/Tony Stone Images; carving at Stanford University by carvers from New Guinea, photo by John Cassidy; bird of paradise plant, ©Ed Reschke/Peter Arnold, Inc. Page 47: from left, houses photo by Gary Johnston; photo of Stephanie Hendry by Gary Johnston; handwriting by Annette Gebben; Papua New Guinean flag. Page 57: photo of Uutsie Apatiki by Lisa Moorehead. Page 58: from left; images from NW Coast button robes, courtesy of the Thomas Burke Memorial Washington State Museum, catalog numbers 25.0146, 1-1654, & 1-1492; walrus mask worn during the Walrus Dance performed by the King Island Dancers at the Alaska Federation of Natives Conference in Anchorage, photo ©Fred Hirschmann; Alaskan boy in traditional ceremonial parka, Barrow, Alaska, photo ©Michael Evan Sewell/Peter Arnold, Inc. Page 59: from left; United States flag; moose in Denali National Park, photo ©Kim Heacox/Tony Stone Images; photo of Uutsie Apatiki by Lisa Moorehead; handwriting by Anne Johnson; polar bear, photo ©David E. Myers/Stock Connection. Page 67: photo of Dermot, John & Colleen Quigley by Crispin Hughes. Page 68: from left, border by Linda Harris; donkey photo by Crispin Hughes; shamrock illustration by Kong Lu; landscape photo by Crispin Hughes; road signs in Killarney, FPG International Corp. Page 69: from left, photo of sign by Crispin Hughes; photo of Colleen Quigley by Crispin Hughes; handwriting by Jill Turney; sheep photo by Crispin Hughes; Irish flag; Clifton cottage along Sky Road, Galway, Ireland, ©1989 E. Nagele/FPG International Corp.; Irish setter, ©Per Eriksson/The Image Bank. Inside back cover: photo of Dermot, John & Colleen Quigley by Crispin Hughes; string photo by Peter Fox.

Dugong

String GAMES

from Around the WORLD

by Anne Akers Johnson 🕷 Klutz Press

Development:
Anne Akers Johnson

Cover Art and Watercolor
Illustrations:
Jessie Hartland

Instructional Drawings:
Sara Boore

Art Direction:
MaryEllen Podgorski

Design and Graphics:
Elizabeth Buchanan

Photo and Art Research:
Marilyn Green

Ridiculous Suggestions:
John Cassidy

Special thanks to Katie Woy.

Published by Klutz Press
Palo Alto, California

Book manufactured in Korea.
String manufactured in Korea.

Acknowledgments and credits appear on page 80.

Write us: Klutz Press is an independent publisher located in Palo Alto, California and staffed entirely by real human beings. We would love to hear your comments regarding this or any of our books.

Klutz Press
2121 Staunton Court
Palo Alto, CA 94306

Additional copies: If you are having trouble locating additional copies of this or other Klutz books, give us a call at (415) 857-0888 for the name of your nearest retailer. Should they be tragically out of stock, additional books can be ordered from our mail order catalogue. See back page.

4 1 5 8 5 7 0 8 8 8

ISBN 1-57054-040-3

Grrrr

LIST of GAMES

NORTH AMERICA

EUROPE ASIA

SOUTH AMERICA

AFRICA

AUSTRALIA

PALM TREE

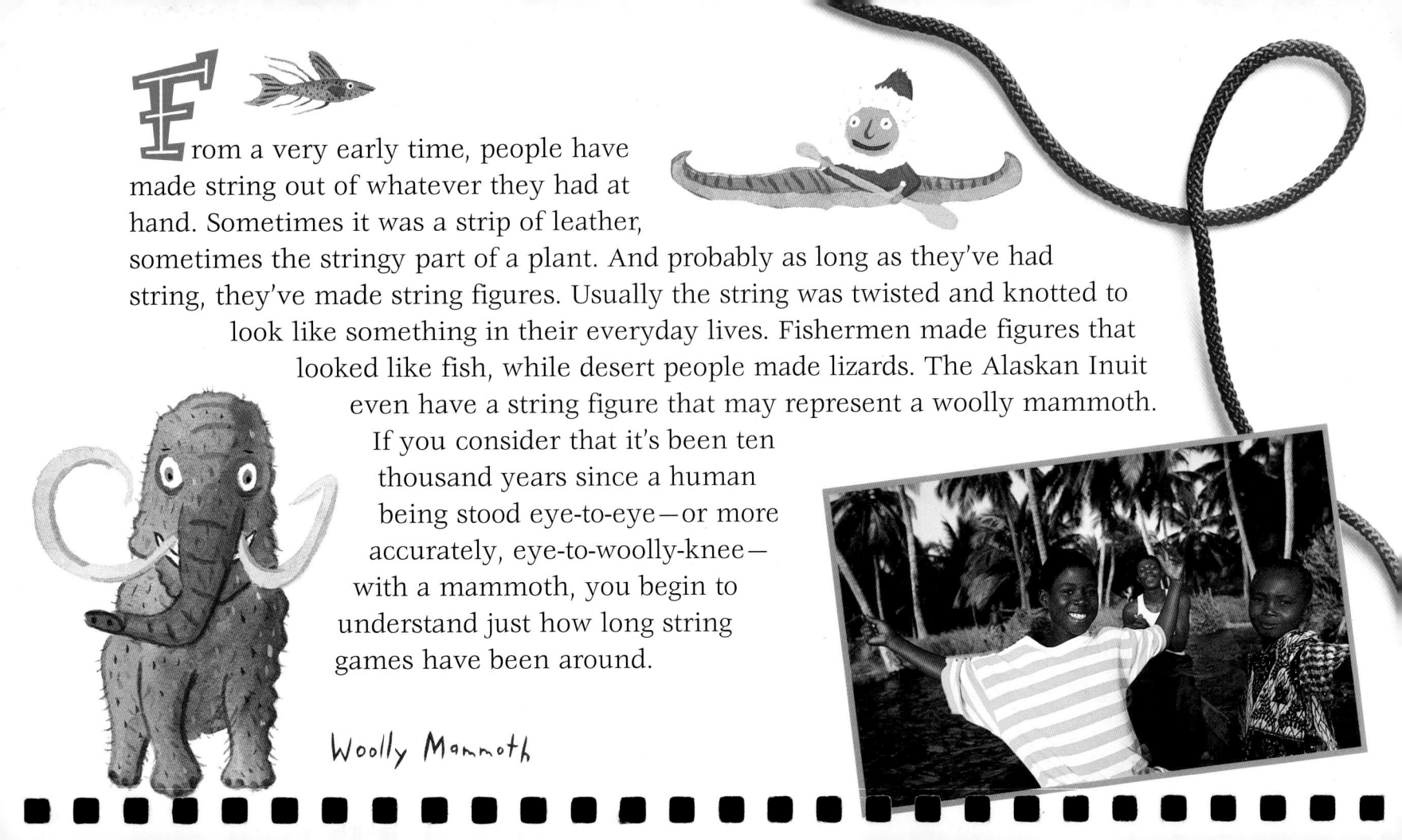

From a very early time, people have made string out of whatever they had at hand. Sometimes it was a strip of leather, sometimes the stringy part of a plant. And probably as long as they've had string, they've made string figures. Usually the string was twisted and knotted to look like something in their everyday lives. Fishermen made figures that looked like fish, while desert people made lizards. The Alaskan Inuit even have a string figure that may represent a woolly mammoth. If you consider that it's been ten thousand years since a human being stood eye-to-eye—or more accurately, eye-to-woolly-knee— with a mammoth, you begin to understand just how long string games have been around.

Woolly Mammoth

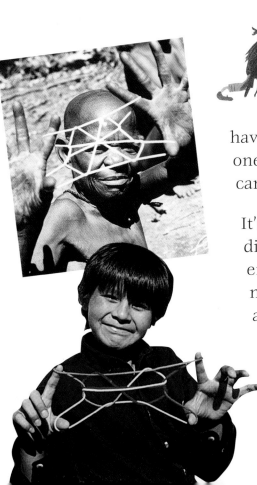

Sometimes the same string figure is found in completely different parts of the world. The African Pygmy woman in this photo is doing pretty much the same figure as the Navajo boy. Of course they probably have different names for this figure. What looks like a fishing spear in one part of the world, might look more like a broom or a bunch of candles in another.

It's hard to say for sure why the same figures pop up in such different parts of the world. Some figures are probably just easy enough that different people invented them on their own. Or maybe they learned new games when travellers from far away passed through town.

In this book, when we tell you where the string game comes from, we're just telling you one of the places it's found. It may in fact be found in very different parts of the world too.

BOLIVIA
BRAZIL
Chacoan Peccary
PARAGUAY
South America
Paraguay
dairy farming
tin roof
Filadelfia
PARAGUAY
Asunción
ARGENTINA
pet Caiman
Toucan